10 Ways
to Prepare Your
Daughter
for Life

Annie Chapman

HARVEST HOUSE PUBLISHERS

EUGENE, OREGON

Unless otherwise indicated, all Scripture quotations are taken from the New American Standard Bible®, © 1960, 1962, 1963, 1968, 1971, 1972, 1973, 1975, 1977, 1995 by The Lockman Foundation. Used by permission.

Verses marked NKJV are taken from the New King James Version. Copyright ©1982 by Thomas Nelson, Inc. Used by permission. All rights reserved.

Verses marked TLB are taken from *The Living Bible*, Copyright © 1971. Used by permission of Tyndale House Publishers, Inc., Wheaton, Illinois 60189. All rights reserved.

Italics in Scripture quotations indicate author's emphasis.

Cover by Dugan Design Group, Bloomington, Minnesota

Cover photos © Diamond Sky Images / Digital Vision / Getty Images; Bigstock / Serg64

10 WAYS TO PREPARE YOUR DAUGHTER FOR LIFE
Copyright © 2002 by Annie Chapman
Published 2012 by Harvest House Publishers
Eugene, Oregon 97402

Library of Congress Cataloging-in-Publication Data
  Chapman, Annie.
    [10 things I want my daughter to know]
    10 ways to prepare your daughter for life / Annie Chapman.
        p. cm.
    Originally published: 10 things I want my daughter to know. ©2002.
    Includes bibliographical references.
    ISBN 978-0-7369-4627-8 (pbk.)
    ISBN 978-0-7369-4628-5 (eBook)
    1. Mothers and daughters—Religious aspects—Christianity. 2. Parenting—Religious aspects—Christianity. 3. Daughters—Religious life. I. Title. II. Title: Ten ways to prepare your daughter for life.

BV4529.18.C435 2012
248.8'33—dc23   2011032580

All rights reserved. No part of this publication may be reproduced, stored in a retrieval system, or transmitted in any form or by any means—electronic, mechanical, digital, photocopy, recording, or any other—except for brief quotations in printed reviews, without the prior permission of the publisher.

Printed in the United States of America

 12 13 14 15 16 17 18 19 20 / BP-SK / 10 9 8 7 6 5 4 3 2 1

To Emmitt and Heidi Beall,
Nathan and Stephanie Chapman,
and all those who come afterward.

Acknowledgments

This book has been graced by the wisdom and insight of many friends who have shared what they learned while shaping their daughters' lives. For their help, I am eternally grateful.

Marie Arritt
Gayle Atwell
Heidi Beall
Tish Beall
Kathy Bently
Kim Bolton
Sherly Bott
Melissa Brown
Velberta Carr
Susie Carson
Lillian Chapman
Alice Click
Joan Cook
Barbara Crook
Becky DeCoy
Nina Elkins
Karen Fletcher
Linda Goodman
Ronda Hardwick

Nancy Harrell
Linda Hershey
Jessica Jones
Jamie Kearney
Marilyn Layton
Jeannie Martin
Teresa Martin
Becky Moore
Kim Napier
Carolyn Norman
Denise Peters
Melody Petrunak
Patsy Powell
Teri Price
Candy Richey
Hazel Slaughter
Kay DeKalb Smith
Hilda Williams
Ilene Wilson

Contents

Bless the Lord, O my soul;
and all that is within me,
bless His holy name.
Psalm 103:1

Introduction

When I brought my sweet baby girl home from the hospital that warm April afternoon, I had no idea what a daunting task I had before me. At the time, all that concerned me was whether my "milk" would come in and I would be able to satisfy her need for nourishment. Since I had been a finicky eater when I was a baby (something I have no recollection of and have managed to successfully overcome to a fault), I was consumed with worry that she would be the same. I was so afraid I would be unable to feed and care for her adequately.

As I stroked her velvety soft skin, traced her rosebud lips with my fingertip, and counted and recounted her ten fingers and ten toes, I was oblivious to all that would be required in the years to follow. God is so good to fill us with such a sense of awe for the miracle of new life that we are able to savor each moment, ignore the enormity of the task, and gladly endure each test.

Now, as I contemplate the 31 years of enjoying my lovely daughter, I see the picture more fully, framed by the years of time. Instead of seeing each brush stroke of instruction, each shading of darks and lights of discipline and guidance, I stand back and observe the beautiful gift and lovely painting her life has become. And that beauty was never more vibrant and evident than the day she got married.

For months, all of my thoughts and all of my efforts revolved around helping Heidi and Emmitt prepare for the anticipated day. The photographer had been secured, the church selected, the florist arranged, and the caterer hired. With reams of yellow legal pads filled, crossed off, and discarded, my life had been one continuous "to do" list. My entire existence was governed by small post 'em notes scattered throughout my kitchen.

The morning of the wedding was different than I had anticipated. There was truly a surreal feeling. Although the advance planning had been emotionally draining, I felt a comforting peace. Previously I had cried a bucket of tears just discussing ideas for the ceremony. I can recall being overcome with emotion while typing out the words, "The doors will open and you will begin to walk down the aisle with your father!" With this as my point of reference, I assumed I would be a complete basket case by the time the processional music started. I could hardly believe the sense of calm I experienced when the actual event unfolded in front of me.

Heidi's curly ebony hair tucked beneath the snow-white veil and her slim waist accenting a beautifully sequined bodice on her long flowing gown were sights I had envisioned with sadness, but now I saw the loveliness of the moment.

As the sanctity of the service proceeded, I looked on as a spectator in the truest sense of the word. Totally out of control of the process that had started, I waited for it to be over, accomplished, finished. I wanted to complete my role of finality, to walk out of the church no longer the mother of a little girl but now a partner in a sisterhood of adult women. And sure enough, it came to pass. Heidi was no longer my baby, she was Emmitt's wife. I knew nothing would ever be the same.

My chance to shape Heidi's life was over. I had more than two decades to do my job, but as I watched her I wondered if I had done enough. Had I prepared her to be the kind of woman she needed to be?

In the following pages I share 10 lessons learned from those years...10 things I wanted to impart to my daughter. My earnest desire is to encourage and assist you who are in the midst of raising girls to be beautiful, godly women. I also hope daughters, who may have been the recipients a generation unmentored by godly mothers, will receive this gentle instruction on how to be complete, strong, effective women.

1

Choices Not Circumstances

Life is not a matter of circumstances,
but issues of choice.
I want my daughter to build her life
on the rock-solid foundation of Christ.
I want to share with her the basics of discernment
and the best ways to make life choices.

There Are No Small Choices

A large billowy cloud of dust barreled up behind them as they roared up the loose gravel and dirt driveway. They skidded to a stop and threw the doors open. Two teenage girls jumped out of a bright red 1967 Barracuda. Janet, beaming from ear to ear, had just received the brand-new car as a "sweet 16" birthday present from her parents. Her friend Sarah, who was one year younger, was just as excited as if it had been her car.

"Come go for a ride with us!" they begged. "Puleeeze!"

My life was considerably different from these two carefree "city" friends. Being a farm girl with chores and responsibilities, I couldn't just jump into a car and ride off. Looking around and seeing no one, I threw caution to the wind and the three of us crowded into the front seat.

At the last minute, Janet and Sarah changed places. Sarah took the driver's side. Unlicensed and inexperienced, she took hold of the stick shift, put the car into reverse, swerved around, and slammed it into forward. Gravel flew as we sped away. Winding around sharp corners at highway speed on the narrow country road proved too much for her to handle. She lost control of the car and, for a brief moment, the Barracuda went airborne before landing in a ditch. The shiny new vehicle came to an abrupt and costly halt. We climbed out of the car and began walking to the nearest house to call our parents.

Up until this moment my choices had not been large ones. Without question, it was foolish of me to get into an unfamiliar, fast car with two inexperienced drivers. However, it was utterly insane of me to *stay* in the car driven by a young, unlicensed person. I was in a pickle, and it was of my own making.

Then I faced another choice that would prove more impacting than the collision I had walked away from. After we got out of the car and realized we were all walking upright, my two friends began to plead, "Please, don't tell anyone it was Sarah driving."

"I'll lose my car," Janet cried. "I'll be arrested," Sarah sobbed. They were relentless in their imploring.

The moment of truth came a few minutes after the arrival of our parents. Sarah's mother came straight to me and asked me point blank, "Who was driving the car?" My choice was obvious: Do I lie and save my relationship and Janet's driving privileges or do I tell the truth?

I replied without hesitation, "Sarah was driving." The mother looked surprisingly relieved. She then said, "I talked to your mother, Annie. She was working in the garden when you three drove by. She told me it was Sarah who was driving. If you had lied to me, I wouldn't have trusted you again."

What a tough day! One good choice and some bad ones. Many years have come and gone since that hot summer afternoon yet the truth remains unchanged. Life is made up of choices great and small. What we eat, what we wear, where we go, and who we see are determinations often made without much thought. I want my daughter to know that although we go through our day unaware of most of the long-term impacts of our choices, the fact is that no decision is insignificant.

My daughter, Heidi, encountered this truth the day Steve and I took her to college. It is forever seared into my heart.

I had apprehensions concerning her leaving home since the moment she was born. In fact, I never wanted either of my children to leave home. Having dreaded this time for so long, the week before taking Heidi to Lee University in Cleveland, Tennessee, was busy and emotionally charged. Packing suitcases wasn't such a change in our routine because we've traveled together as a family to give concerts all of our lives. What I found unsettling, though, was the storing of Heidi's favorite momentos and pictures. It felt as though we were erasing her childhood. The job was completed, and "the day" arrived.

We arrived at the university with a minimal amount of trauma. By the time Steve and I were supposed to leave, the schedule for Heidi's classes was completed and her dorm room was in order. After multiple hugs and kisses, Heidi stood on the sidewalk watching as we got into our car. It was then I saw her veneer start to crack. Tears filled her eyes as she sadly whispered, "Why did I think I could do this? I don't want to stay here."

Oh, my! Time seemed to stand still as Heidi and I locked in a mother/daughter gaze. As we looked at each other, I couldn't help but think back to those early-morning feeding rendezvous when she was an infant. With her soft skin and deep-blue eyes, she had owned my heart. Now, here we were 18 years later, and despite the usual spats and conflicts that came with time and gender I realized she was forever a part of me. We were both at a loss for words, and the hour had come for us to make choices:

> I had to decide not to open the car door and beckon my sweet baby to come home with her mommy because love demanded I cut the maternal cord. Heidi had to choose to set aside her fears and bravely walk away from her parents.

As painful as that choice was for Heidi, it is one that proved more important than she realized at the time. The decision to stay that day changed her life forever. Within hours of choosing the difficult over the comfortable, she met a darling young man named Emmitt—whom she married two years later.

Of course that day in the parking lot of Lee University was not the first important decision Heidi had made. Life-changing choices had begun years before.

I Want My Daughter to Choose Heaven

The first and most important goal I set as a mother was to make sure my daughter understood the blessed gift God had provided through the finished work of Jesus Christ on the cross. Each night as Heidi was preparing for bed we would talk about God.

I answered questions about who He was and why He did things the way He did. I tried to come up with adequate answers about why the sky is blue and if baby fishes have to wait 30 minutes after they eat before they can go swimming. We also tackled the harder issues such as "why Grandma has cancer" and "why Heidi's cousin Aimee died when she wanted to live so badly." At the end of such probing discussions I would occasionally ask Heidi if she wanted to ask Jesus into her heart and let Him, as she would put it, be "the boss in her brain." Then one night, to my delight, she said yes. We prayed a simple sinner's prayer—one that a five year old could comprehend.

When a child is so young, it's not always easy to know if the salvation prayer is a sincere desire to surrender his or her life to Christ or just a way to please an eager mother. That question was soon answered for me. A few weeks after Heidi had prayed to receive Christ, Steve and I were rejoicing over the fact that a friend of ours had trusted Christ as his Savior. I turned to Heidi and asked if she would like to pray and give her heart to Jesus.

She stood up and looked at me as only she can. With her dimpled hands perched on her hips and her curly topped head cocked to one side in exasperation, she said, "Mommy! Don't you remember? I already asked Jesus into my heart—and He came in!" That's all I needed to know.

Another Faith Choice

When our children were young, our family attended Belmont Church in Nashville, Tennessee. It was a vibrantly alive body of believers we loved dearly. However, there was one small inconvenience. Since the building was really old, it had a baptismal pool that resembled a watery tomb from the Dark Ages. It looked quite intimidating and the acoustics inside created eerie echoes when people spoke. Nonetheless, this was where the church members "buried the old man" through baptism.

After a time of instruction, Heidi decided she wanted to be baptized—except for one little hindrance. She had observed something that caused her great trepidation when her brother was baptized a few months earlier. When the church officials opened the baptismal tomb, she had noticed a huge water bug floating on the surface. To a rather timid little girl, this nautical insect was just enough of a deterrent to frighten her away from this holy sacrament.

I could tell she was struggling over the issue because she spoke often of the dreaded creepy crawler. Steve and I didn't push the idea of her being baptized. But having seen her brother take the step and understanding, as much as possible, the importance of that act of obedience, she kept steady pressure on herself.

Finally, one day when we were driving in the car, she announced that she had made the choice to be "dunked."

Our family, along with a few close friends, went to the church. As the men cracked open the iron doors to the watery sepulcher she looked on with anxious eyes. Thankfully, to everyone's relief, there was no bug. The look of relaxation was quite evident on Heidi's face as she joyfully submitted to this step of faith and obedience.

I Want My Daughter to Choose Happiness

Joy and contentment are born out of an attitude that is grown from the inside and shows on the outside. It is true that circumstances can make us feel helpless, but *happiness is always a choice*. From my own experience I know how crucial this attitude is to adopt.

Steve and I were enroute to a concert weekend in Pennsylvania. Our day had started at 4 A.M., and we were not expected to arrive at our destination until late that evening. All I could think about was getting to our hotel room, taking a nice hot bath, and going to sleep. We had also traveled many weekends in a row, most of them with two small children, so I was very, very tired.

As we drove toward the town, I mentioned to Steve my eagerness to get to the hotel. Reluctantly, he told me we would be staying in a home arranged by the man sponsoring the concert. Steve knew this was not the best situation, but the home accommodations had been offered to us and he felt an obligation to accept.

Usually we love making new friends and experiencing the value of getting to know folks in a deeper way. But there's one fundamental problem with this housing arrangement. Invariably, we talk much too late into the night and don't get the rest we need to function properly the next day. I knew when Steve told me the situation, my day was far from over. I was going to have to be "nice" to these people, and I wasn't sure if there was any "nice" left in me.

Steve could tell I was upset. Instead of making the choice to "get over it," I began to tumble further and further into a place in my mind that left me depressed and feeling desolate. There's no logical explanation as to why I let it go so far, but I did. By the time we got to our lodging, I felt hurt, unloved, and angry. To put even more pressure on myself, I hid these feelings and "played" nice.

In retrospect, I know I allowed myself to be plunged into the depths of despair over something that was very insignificant. If I had chosen to accept the situation as it was instead of nursing the disappointment and blaming Steve, my weekend could have turned out quite differently. Unfortunately, I let myself be upset for days. It made no difference that the family we stayed with had been delightful and very conscious of our need for privacy.

Since then I have discovered four things that are needed to make the right choice.

Be Aware

To continue with my lodging story, in the midst of it all, I felt like a dirty rotten sinner because I was unable to "shake off the sad and put on the glad." As hard as I tried, I couldn't "Pollyanna" my way back to reality. That's the bad news. The good news is that a logical explanation exists for my struggle. I have come to realize that sometimes our sad, lonely feelings have little to do with our lack of spiritual maturity and more to do with being physically exhausted. Looking back on that weekend, I realize I was overworked and burned out from traveling continuously with two small children. This left me weak and vulnerable to the fiery darts of the enemy.

The prophet Elijah is a perfect example of one who suffered spiritually because of being physical spent. Recapping his day, which is chronicled in 1 Kings 19, leaves me gasping for breath and reaching for a Dr Pepper and a Snickers.

First, Elijah was involved in an intense spiritual battle with King Ahab. In that encounter Elijah had victoriously proven the superiority of Jehovah God over the false gods of Baal. Then he took a sword and killed nearly 900 false prophets. If that weren't enough, he went into deep prayer and intercession, asking God to end the three-year drought that had plagued the country of Israel.

Upon receiving an affirmative answer from God that He was indeed going to send rain, Elijah took off on foot and ran 20 miles to get back to Jezreel in advance of the king (who was riding in a chariot).

After all that, Elijah's day was still far from over. When Jezebel, the king's wife, heard that all of the pagan prophets were dead and it was Elijah who killed them, she sent word to him that she would take revenge by killing him within 24 hours. He knew she was capable of doing it, so he immediately took off again, this time running for his life. The journey from Jezreel to Beersheba is nearly a week's journey on foot. When he arrived in Beersheba, he went another 20 miles or so into the desert.

Is it any wonder Elijah, this great man of faith and courage, lost the will to live? First Kings 19:4 says, "And he came and sat down under a juniper tree; and he requested for himself that he might die." Does it sound like he'd lost his faith in God? In verse 5 we see what was really wrong with him: "He lay down and slept under a juniper tree; and behold, there was an angel touching him, and he said to him, 'Arise, eat.'" Then Elijah went back to sleep. The angel awakened him again and said, "Arise, eat, because the journey is too great for you." Was Elijah backslidden? No! He was tired and hungry. No amount of prayer was going to fix what food and sleep could do for him.

If someone as spiritually close to God as Elijah got depressed to the place of despairing of life, then should we be surprised when we are waylaid by physical and spiritual exhaustion? We need to be aware of our situation and what led to it, whether it be sin or exhaustion.

Be Thankful

An ungrateful, selfish heart always leaves us feeling miserable. With this attitude, no matter what we have, it is never enough. I once read "happiness is a choice; misery is optional." How true! God's Word tells us how to avoid that pain. He says, "In everything give thanks; for this is God's will for you in Christ Jesus" (1 Thessalonians 5:18).

Do you recall this scene from the movie *The Hiding Place?* In addition to all the tormenting conditions women had to deal with in the Nazi concentration camps, one of them was dealing with the infestation of lice in the sleeping barracks. Corrie ten Boom's sister, Betsie, was telling the prisoners about the love and mercy of God. Corrie, listening to her sister's teaching, but struggling to make sense of the suffering God had allowed in her life through the hands of the Nazis, bitterly declared to her sister, "I will not be thankful for the lice." Then one day, while Betsie was sharing the Word of God, Corrie realized the reason the guards were not coming into the sleeping area of the prisoners: They didn't want to be exposed to the lice! The truth of the gospel could be preached to these dying women *because* of the lice.

God in His divine power "causes all things to work together for good to those who love God, to those who are called according to His purpose" (Romans 8:28).

Be Selective

When we allow our joy to be stolen over something insignificant we waste our sorrows. That's why it's so critical to distinguish between what is important and what is not so important. Galatians 6:9 says, "Let us not lose heart in doing good, for in due time we will reap if we do not grow weary." Happiness is not always getting what we want. As an example, let me share how Heidi learned this hard lesson. When the movie *Titanic* came out quite a few years ago, our family was genuinely excited about seeing it. We had enjoyed the old black-and-white version and were intrigued with the storyline. Since Heidi was born on April 15, the date of the sinking of the ship, she was especially fascinated. •

We were all set to go see the film when we heard about the bad language and the illicit sexual overtones of the movie. We decided it wasn't a suitable family movie. To say Heidi was bitterly disappointed would be a serious understatement. She convinced herself that she could not be truly happy until she saw the film. As the time approached for her birthday, she became more and more obsessed with seeing the movie.

Steve and I tried to appease her need for a *Titanic* fix. We took her to Orlando, Florida, where they had an incredible exhibition of the actual artifacts that had been salvaged from the wreckage. (All right, I admit we were singing in Orlando anyway, but we did take the time to attend.) On another occasion in Nashville, Steve took Heidi to a fancy restaurant in town that had a special reenactment (minus the iceberg and the massive loss of life) of the fateful night of the sinking of the great ship. The two of them dressed up in early-1900s costumes and shared a once-in-a-lifetime evening. We thought we had helped quench Heidi's thirst for all things *Titanic*, but we were wrong.

Because she turned 18 that birthday, she was feeling old enough to set her own standards for movie-going, which challenged our standard that any movie that takes God's name in vain is unacceptable for viewing. Heidi came home one evening and announced, as boldly as she could with her chin quivering, that she had gone to see the epic film despite our objections. Disappointed in her choice, I asked only one question: "Did it make you happy?"

As she looked at the hurt expression on her father's face, she burst into tears. "No," she replied. "I hated it. I can't believe I made such a big deal over such a stupid movie." Then we all cried together.

Heidi asked God to forgive her, not just because she wasted her evening, disrespected her parents, squandered her money, or got suckered in by the hype of the movie industry, but also because she chose to give something so unimportant as a movie such power in her life. She had made it an idol and, in the process, disappointed those who love her.

Life is full of choices that promise joy but do not produce. The lasting happiness we seek cannot be acquired from the world. We can't drink it, smoke it, chew it, dip it, buy it, or eat it. The song that says "the world didn't give it to me, and the world can't take it away" surely applies to the pursuit of happiness. Only God can fill that empty spot in our hearts and teach us that blissfulness is *choosing to practice the joy of the Lord*. This is developed in our hearts by choosing the right attitude and realizing our circumstances do not have to determine whether we're going to experience the happiness we seek. Matthew 5:6 reminds us, "Blessed are those who hunger and thirst for righteousness, for they shall be satisfied."

Be Positive

When we choose to see life as a "glass half full rather than half empty," we change the power our circumstances have over our lives. In fact, a pastor once said a Christian's face should be a living advertisement for the world to see. A cheerful smile and happy demeanor announce, "There is a God, and He is full of love and mercy toward you." Proverbs 15:13 and 17:22 remind us of the necessity of cultivating a good sense of humor about life: "A joyful heart makes a cheerful face, but when the heart is sad, the spirit is broken"; "a joyful heart is good medicine, but a broken spirit dries up the bones." And Philippians 4:8 says, "Brethren, whatever is true, whatever is honorable, whatever is right, whatever is pure, whatever is lovely, whatever is of good repute, if there is any excellence and if anything worthy of praise, dwell on these things."

I Want My Daughter to Choose Health

Here's a bit of wisdom I have shared with Heidi throughout her life: *Don't let anything you can change limit your life.* I discovered this ancient truth back in 1974, the year before Steve and I married. At the time I was working at Teen Haven, a youth center in the inner city of Philadelphia. It was established for the purpose of ministering to the people in the neighborhood. I lived with other staff members in a row house on North Broad Street. We taught the children to read and conducted Bible studies in local homes. During the summer, we took the children and teenagers to a camp located in Lancaster County, about an hour and a half outside Philadelphia. As part of the full-time staff, one of my responsibilities was to prepare the meals for the 30 or so people who had come from colleges across the country to assist with the work for the summer. I also helped with the cooking (for around 120 people) at the camp when the campers were present.

Being in the kitchen surrounded by food most of my day highlighted an ongoing personal problem. It was an issue God wanted to work on. Since my late childhood and into my adolescent years, I had a considerable weight problem. In my book *Letting Go of Anger,* I share more details of the "whys" of that struggle, but the heart of the matter is that I used food as a comforting, self-medicating solution to my woundedness. By the summer of '74, I was approximately 75 pounds overweight. I used weight like an overcoat to insulate me from men. It protected me, but it also left me feeling defeated and worthless. One day while I was reading my Bible, I came across this passage in 2 Peter 2:19: "For by what a person is overcome, by this he is enslaved."

Such a simple verse, and yet this was the Word of truth God chose to use as an instrument of power in my life. I started looking at what all I had allowed to enslave me. One of the most vicious of all taskmasters was *food.* It was this realization that helped me start to make wiser choices.

Up until that time, I felt hopeless when it came to the weight issue. I had overcome many difficulties in my life, but this was the problem that controlled me. Part of the hopelessness was believing I had gone too far. Any effort to change the situation seemed futile. With so much weight to lose, I concluded, "It doesn't matter if I eat this cookie, or this bag of chips, or this quart of ice cream. Look at me, I'm so fat I'm beyond help."

With God's power, however, I began to look at each "choice" opportunity one at a time and make my decision a good one. If I wanted to eat a cookie, I would look at it as my "slave master." I would ask myself, "Is this what I want to rule my life?" I was letting something I was capable of changing *run* and *ruin* my life.

With a whole new committed determination, I chose to take my health back!

Within a year's time, I shed 60 pounds. I didn't follow a specific plan, I simply made the commitment that each morsel of food would be one that was good for my body. I began to move around more. Instead of being a couch potato I started walking. Exercise became something that made me feel healthy instead of just being a necessary evil.

Weight might not be your issue. But regardless of what your weak area is, Hebrews 12:1 tells us, "Let us also lay aside every encumbrance and the sin which so easily entangles us, and let us run with endurance the race that is set before us."

I want Heidi to remember that our choices determine our destination. I want her to choose heaven, choose happiness, and choose health. If she has these three she has it all.

2

Beauty or Beast?

I want my daughter to know
she needs to be the best
representation for her Creator
in her appearance and demeanor.

Being Pretty Inside and Outside

One day while homeschooling Heidi, I asked her what "casualty" means. She thought for a moment, then said, "It's when you don't really dress up, but you're not dressed sloppily either." Personal appearance is something my daughter has thought about often, even when she should have been thinking about other things. And she's not alone. This is one subject that occupies the thoughts of most women, young and old.

One day while driving along in my minivan, I scanned through the various radio programs. As I paused long enough to let a country song play, I was amused. The refrain went something like this: "She ain't pretty, she just looks that way." Leave it to a clever songwriter to tell it like it is. How many people have you met whose outward attractiveness was appealing and totally captivating? However, after getting further acquainted with them their external beauty faded to invisible.

Of course, the opposite effect of a person's appearance has also occurred. When I was in junior high school I had an English teacher I thought was the most homely person I had ever met. Reflecting back on her appearance, I can't for the life of me remember what I deemed so unlovely. Nonetheless, as the days went by and she taught me to open my heart and mind to the exciting world of literature, her appearance changed. Amazingly, with each passing day she grew more and more beautiful. Now some four decades later when I recall my 12 years of pre-college school experience, she stands out as the best and most lovely of all my instructors. What changed? Her physical characteristics remained the same; yet, I saw her differently. Having been privileged to be around her long enough, I finally noticed her true beauty.

The Beauty Game Is an Ugly Business

"Pretty" is very culturally defined. Throughout the centuries different physical attributes have been valued over others. Take a look at the encyclopedia pictures of the full-figured women posing in the Renaissance period with their big thighs, round bellies, and small breasts. (Oh, for the good ol' days! The women depicted in the portraits were the super-models of their era, and I would have fit right in with them.)

Today the style is different and opens the doors to unhealthy behavior. In order to combat the negative pressure put on our daughters to look like the models in magazines and on television, it might be a good idea to get those old books down from the shelves and show them the Cindy Crawfords and the Brittany Spears' of those days.

The current standards of acceptable beauty are difficult to escape. The reed-thin waiflike bodies, wide eyes, small round chins, and big breasts grace the covers of nearly every periodical. Beauty hasn't changed—only the specific aspect each generation chooses to reward.

One gift a mother can give a daughter is *knowledge*. As you look at the cover of magazines, do your daughter a favor. Discuss with her the role of computer enhancements and air brushing. The perfection she thinks she sees when she looks at the beautiful faces and bodies is a mirage. They don't really exist.

In an article on how cover photos are doctored by the publishers, a reporter revealed that even the pictures of models as young as 16 years old had wrinkles and imperfections that had to be air-brushed out. Any flaws were erased through the use of computers. If the youngest and most perfect of the models was not acceptable without artificial corrections, how can our young ones stand up to the pressure of looking like these girls and women? The unrealistic nature of the "beauty industry" must be challenged. The magazine companies who make their living selling unattainable fantasies will not be the ones to do it. As the mothers and mentors of young women in our trust, we must take exception to the industry's definition of beauty. If we don't, our sweet little girls will grow up feeling inadequate and less than the beautiful, wondrous creations God made.

How do we teach our daughters the true meaning and purpose of beauty in this appearance-crazed culture? Let's start with the Word of God and see where true beauty originates and how it is maintained. Isaiah 3:16-24 is quite a lengthy passage concerning the attitude of true beauty:

> Moreover, the Lord said, "Because the daughters of Zion are proud and walk with heads held high and seductive eyes, and go along with mincing steps and tinkle the bangles on their feet, therefore the Lord will afflict the scalp of the daughters of Zion with scabs, and the Lord will make their foreheads bare." In that day the Lord will take away the beauty of their anklets, headbands, crescent ornaments, dangling earrings, bracelets, veils, headdresses, ankle chains, sashes, perfume boxes, amulets, finger rings, nose rings, festal robes, outer tunics, cloaks, money purses, hand mirrors, undergarments, turbans, and veils.

> Now it will come about that instead of sweet perfume there will be putrefaction; instead of a belt, a rope; instead of well-set hair, a plucked-out scalp; instead of fine clothes, a donning of sackcloth; and branding instead of beauty.

Sounds pretty serious! Why is God so judgmental of this outward display of beauty? In this passage judgment is coming to God's people. The emphasis on the outward manifestations of pride and arrogance are demonstrated by the over-attention to the exterior appearance. There is nothing wrong with the outward adornment described in these verses, but there is something terribly wrong when all of the emphasis is on the external and the heart is neglected. God again warns of this imbalance in 1 Peter 3:3-5:

> Your adornment must not be merely external—braiding the hair, and wearing gold jewelry, or putting on dresses; but let it be the *hidden person of the heart*, with the imperishable quality of a gentle and quiet spirit, which is precious in the sight of God. For in this way in former times the holy women also, who hoped in God, used to adorn themselves...

The contrast between outward and inner beauty continues in 1 Timothy 2:9,10:

> Likewise, I want women to adorn themselves with proper clothing, modestly and discreetly, not with braided hair and gold or pearls or costly garments, but rather by means of good works, as is proper for women making a claim to godliness.

The way we dress and act announces to people around us who we really are. We must not allow our standards of modesty and discretion to be subject to the whims of fashion or popular culture.

A Mother's Responsibility

At the time of this writing, many popular music artists are known for their vulgar, skimpy outfits, their numerous plastic surgery enhancements, and the swivel capacity and sexual moves of their bodies. If all the women musicians were doing was exploiting themselves, that would be tragic enough. However, it is horrifying to realize the average age of their fan base is 8- to 9-year-old girls. This may sound like I'm an old fuddy-duddy but look at the "fruit" of allowing such entertainment in our homes. Is it any wonder that children are acting out sexually at younger and younger ages when their pop culture idols practically simulate sexual relations on stage under the disguise of a concert or video performance? If we allow our daughters to be inundated with these images and messages, should we really be surprised when they do what they see?

I wish the sexual exploitation in the entertainment industry was uncommon. Unfortunately, the marketplace is saturated with it. As an informed mother, find a way to preview the music videos your daughter will see. This kind of hands-on involvement will require time, effort, and courage on your part. However, it is time and energy wisely invested in your daughter's well being. If your daughter is old enough, screen part of the video together and discuss why it is unacceptable viewing. On those occasions when the video is contrary to the acceptable moral standards of the family, lovingly confront your daughter with the truth. Offer an alternative if possible. Bake cookies together, look at family photos, go for a walk, or go shopping. These activities serve as a fun distraction and provide a great time of mother–daughter bonding.

While restricting what your child watches in your home is effective, we must also counter popular culture's invasive emphasis on sex. Use your moral guideline talks to stress the importance of modesty in all areas—including the practicalities of day-to-day choices. For instance, what does God require of us when it comes to instructing our daughters in the proper way to dress? In the Greek language of the New Testament, the word for proper is *kosmios,* which indicates we are to *voluntarily* place limitations on ourselves. This means we are to be sensible and self-controlled. Teaching our daughters that true beauty is something that originates within and shines outwardly is vital to their well-being.

Advice from Women Who Know

What do some beautiful women have to say about teaching our daughters the importance of inward and outward beauty? The following ideas come from their wealth of experience.

1. There is nothing wrong with altering something that really bothers you. I know people have different attitudes about cosmetic surgery, but this is something that has to be dealt with between the individual and God. There's nothing wrong with getting braces, contact lenses, having your hair permed or straightened. If you need to change something, do it. If it can't be changed, then learn to deal with it in a different way. I love the well-known prayer, "Lord, grant me the serenity to change the things I can change, to accept the things I cannot change, and the wisdom to know the difference."

2. The heart is where true beauty blooms and brings forth fragrance. Don't spend so much time on the outward that you neglect to cultivate the heart.

3. Psalm 139 says, "I will give thanks to You [God], for I am fearfully and wonderfully made." God does all things well, and our job is to agree with Him.

4. Being content with our appearance brings about our inner beauty that time and age cannot take away.

5. Ephesians 5:29 says, "For no one ever hated his own flesh, but nourishes and cherishes it...." If we look into the mirror and are not pleased with what we see, perhaps the lack of contentment is the result of having distorted what God made.

6. Take good care of your body; it is the temple of the Holy Spirit.

7. Pray and ask Jesus to shine through you so when people look at you, they will see the beauty of Christ in you. Determine to be "others" oriented rather than "me" centered.

8. Don't mar your bodies with permanent fads such as tattoos and piercings.

9. If you are dirty on the inside with sin, no amount of makeup will make you feel good.

10. A sweet spirit (attitude) makes you look beautiful; a nasty attitude makes anyone look ugly.

11. When is it too young to wear makeup? Use wisdom when deciding the appropriate time and amount your daughter can wear. Unless it is an extreme problem, for example the gothic look or the wearing of immoral attire, don't allow makeup to be the "hill on which you are willing to die." Other more important issues will arise in the years to come. Relax and try to compromise without bloodshed or shattered relationships.

12. Learn to use makeup correctly. Once you've decided it's time for your daughter to start wearing makeup, go together to the mall and have a simple makeup consultation with an expert at the cosmetic counter. It doesn't cost very much (usually they just want you to buy one of the makeup items), and it will certainly be worth it in the long run.

13. Remember no matter how beautiful you may be, it is only temporary. For instance, even face lifts have to be repeated in a few years.

14. The world saw a beautiful, wealthy, famously appealing movie star named "Marilyn Monroe." But when she looked into the mirror she must have seen a sad and wounded "Norma Jean Baker." Her tragic suicide is evidence of the inadequacy of outward beauty to bring inner peace.

15. You can enhance the beauty God has given you or you can destroy it, but ultimately it was designed to be used to bring glory to God.

Consider this story about the daughter of one of the royal families of Europe. She had a big, bulbous nose that destroyed her beauty in the eyes of others, but especially in her own. She grew up with a terrible image of herself as an ugly person. Her family hired a plastic surgeon to change the shape of her nose. He did the work, and there came the moment when they took off the bandages and the girl could see the results.

When the doctor removed the dressing, he saw that the operation had been a total success. All the ugly contours were gone. Her nose was different. As soon as the incisions healed and the redness disappeared, she would be a beautiful girl. He held a mirror up for the girl to see. But so deeply embedded was this girl's ugly image of herself that when she saw herself in the mirror, she couldn't see any change. She broke into tears and cried out, "Oh, I knew it wouldn't work!"[1]

The young girl's problem was no longer *how she looked*, but how *she saw herself*. The moral of this story is simple: Don't concentrate on the outside believing it will fix what's wrong on the inside.

Building Confidence

I recall a day when Heidi and I were shopping at the local mall. Heidi was around ten at the time. She saw some girls standing in a group talking. Although she didn't know them, she thought she knew what they were thinking. She said to me, "Mom, those girls think I'm fat."

Of course, there was no way Heidi could have possibly known what the girls were thinking or saying, yet she projected her own dissatisfaction with her appearance onto total strangers. At the time, Heidi was about 15 pounds overweight for her age and height. I could sense we were approaching a potential problem in her life. We stopped right there in the mall and talked about the observation she had just made concerning the group of girls.

I could have tried convincing her that she was wrong, that the girls were not talking and thinking about her. However, it would not have addressed the real problem. The dilemma was not what "they" were thinking, but what Heidi thought of herself.

That day we developed a strategy for changing what was bothering Heidi. She didn't like being overweight and yet at her young age she didn't have the maturity to make the adjustments to her diet and exercise. We made a pact to stay on a sensible program. By the end of the summer Heidi had lost the excess weight and found a sense of contentment with her body. She no longer worried about what others were thinking. (And I dropped a few unnecessary pounds myself!)

The truth is difficult to handle at times, but believing a lie can be even harder to overcome. A pastor's three-year-old daughter, Melissa, came home from Sunday school one day and said, "Nobody likes me in the whole world." Her parents said to her, "Darling, you know we care about you. Why did you say, 'Nobody likes you in the whole world'?" Melissa answered, "My teacher told me." They couldn't believe it. Who would tell a three-year-old child that no one likes him or her? They later discovered the teacher really said, "Melissa, there's nobody like you in the whole world!"[2]

There is great damage in errant thinking. *What we believe shapes how we feel* about ourselves sometimes even more than the truth does. How many of us go through life wounded and maimed not because of what someone actually said or did, but what we perceived he or she had done. It is for the purpose of knowing the truth that we must saturate our minds with God's Word, the ultimate authority. To build confidence and self-assurance in our daughters we need to address their insecurities and problems *and* help them discover their worth in God's eyes.

I lift my daughter in prayer that the truth of God's love and acceptance will be firmly planted in her heart and mind so she can continue to develop the God-given beauty of a gentle and quiet spirit. I am confident she will let her outward appearance reflect the mercy and grace of God in all true loveliness.

3

Pure in Heart and Body

❧

I want my daughter to know that
God created her to walk in a responsible,
morally pure manner. I want her to understand
that her body is the temple of the Holy Spirit.

What's a Nice Girl like You Doing in a Place like This?

It was an exciting evening as the slow, steady rain pelted my leather coat. It's amazing how dark it can seem at 6:30 on a late November day. Despite the darkness of the hour and the gloomy ambiance of the rain, the English cottage was ablaze with lights and a warm, inviting fire burned in the fireplace. About 80 people had gathered to celebrate the marriage of Heidi and Emmitt that would take place the next day. Some of the group assembled were members of the wedding party who had just arrived from a successful rehearsal. They were joining a number of close friends and family for the prewedding celebration of two young lives eager to participate in the awesome mystery of being joined in the holiness of matrimony.

The company was excellent. The slide program showing the bride and groom's earlier years flashed before our eyes at blinding speed. The food was delicious, the pictures touching, and the songs were precious—but it was the words of the bride and grooms' friends that gripped my heart.

One by one college friends and roommates stood and spoke through catching throats and tear-dampened eyes of how they had been impacted by the wise choices Heidi and Emmitt had made in the area of moral purity. Time after time the word "sacrifice" surfaced as they spoke of their own determination to live out their godly ideals.

One of Heidi's friends stood and said, "I've finally seen how a person is supposed to conduct herself in a dating situation so God is honored. After watching Heidi and Emmitt, I've determined from this point on to do it right. I want to do it the way they've done it. I want to date without regrets."

And Heidi and Emmitt had indeed maintained a good testimony of moral rightness amid the temptations that faced them. By the words of the testimonials offered, it made a difference in the lives of those who observed their choices.

Encouraging Purity

I want my daughter to listen to the warning God gives to us concerning those who give themselves over to sensuality. Verses 18 and 19 of 2 Peter 2 say:

> For speaking out arrogant words of vanity they entice by fleshly desires, by sensuality, those who barely escape from the ones who live in error, promising them freedom while they themselves are slaves of corruption; *for by what a man is overcome, by this he is enslaved.*

There are several unique words used in the Bible that deal with the nature of the battle for purity. Some of these terms may be unfamiliar or confusing. For instance, "lasciviousness" is used in Galatians 5:19. Some translations use the more common word "sensuality": "Now the deeds of the flesh are evident, which are: immorality, impurity, sensuality [lasciviousness]....I forewarn you, just as I have forewarned you, that those who practice such things will not inherit the kingdom of God" (Galatians 5:19,21).

Sensuality means "to be preoccupied with bodily and sexual pleasures." And our culture certainly promotes this! Turn on any daytime soap opera or primetime sitcom and the majority of the conversations and activities are given over to acting sensually without shame and without any concern of what others think or how they are affected.

Second Peter 2:2 continues to warn us of the danger of giving ourselves over to uncontrolled sexual impulses: "Many will follow their sensuality, and because of them the way of the truth will be maligned; and in their greed they will exploit you with false words; their judgment from long ago is not idle; and their destruction is not asleep."

Another word used to indicate the degrees of sexual temptation is "concupiscence" or "lust." While sensuality (or lasciviousness) depicts an *attitude*, concupiscence goes one step farther. Lust in this context is a craving that demands an action in order to satisfy desire. It is the fruit of an out-of-control sexual appetite. First Thessalonians 4:4,5 provides God's instructions regarding sexuality: "That each of you know how to possess his own vessel in sanctification and honor, not in lustful passion, like the Gentiles who do not know God."

Romans 6:12,13 says: "Therefore do not let sin reign in your mortal body so that you obey its lusts, and do not go on presenting the members of your body to sin as instruments of unrighteousness; but present yourselves to God as those alive from the dead, and your members as instruments of righteousness to God."

The third word a wise young woman should give heed to is "defraud." Of all the warnings, this is the most important one for daughters to understand. As I heard in a Bill Gothard conference, to "defraud" means to *arouse sexual desires* in another person that cannot be righteously fulfilled. Our girls need to be aware that the way they dress, move, touch, talk, and the attitude they exude can generate desires in men that may lead them down the path to sin.

Females have an enormous amount of power over males. Girls *do* have the ability to stir boys up to the point of spiritual and sexual pain. If we abuse men by deliberately arousing them, God will hold us responsible for the sin of defrauding. It isn't cute, and it isn't fun. It's sin. First Thessalonians 4:6-8 is a sobering warning: "And that no man transgress and defraud his brother in the matter [sexual immorality] because the Lord is the avenger in all these things, just as we also told you before and solemnly warned you. For God has not called us for the purpose of impurity, but in sanctification. Consequently, he who rejects this is not rejecting man but the God who gives His Holy Spirit to you."

The fourth word to explore is "fornication." First Thessalonians 4:3 is a clear directive: "For this is the will of God, your sanctification; that is, that you abstain from sexual immorality."

Some of our young daughters are seeking God for His will in regard to their future vocation, marriage, and ministry. While we can't tell them what God wants them to pursue, we do know for sure what His will is for their lives concerning dating. Sexual immorality must be avoided. Long before a young lady faces the situation of choosing to "go all the way," her attitudes, appetites, and actions need to be brought under the submission of Christ's Lordship. If sensuality, lust, and defrauding are nipped in the bud, then fornication will not even be a possibility.

If your daughter has already encountered problems in this area, reassure her that the spiritual aspects of purity can be restored by our forgiving Savior who can unlock the hurt and liberate love. The woman who has failed in this area still has hope. Galatians 5:1 is a marvelous declaration: "It was for freedom that Christ set us free; therefore keep standing firm and do not be subject again to a yoke of slavery." Verses 13 and 14 continue this thought: "For you were called to freedom, brethren; only do not turn your freedom into an opportunity for the flesh, but through love serve one another. For the whole Law is fulfilled in one word, in the statement, 'You shall love your neighbor as yourself.'"

There is a song my husband and I have performed for many years. The first verse says: "To come into the presence of the Living Lord is to be changed. We cannot come into His high and holy place and stay the same."³ While there is great peace and assurance in God's presence, there is also the painful part of His glorious light exposing the dark, dirty places in our lives. His presence shows us where we need to change. And God also provides the power to do the changing. His light offers warmth and illumination to our lives.

Mothers Give Advice on Moral Decisions

I want to teach my daughter that the choice to follow God in the area of moral purity affects the people around her. I asked some mothers who participated in a survey on dating to share advice they've given to their daughters and also the counsel they have received in the area of dating. Here are some of their words of wisdom and practical advice to help achieve purity.

1. Even though my daughters are still relatively young, I've talked to them since they were five and six years old about *choosing not to date.* I want them to know they should not only save their bodies for marriage, but also I've taken it a step further and encouraged them to protect their hearts from being fragmented by casual dating. Young girls are too quick to become emotionally involved before they have the maturity to handle their feelings.

2. In years past there has been a lot of attention given to *remaining a virgin.* Well, I want my daughter to know that purity and virginity can be two different things. She needs to know that a young girl can be a virgin in name only. Virginity, the mere technicality that she has avoided penetration, should not be her goal. She needs to realize that her hymen can be intact, but her heart can be torn by bad choices. The repercussions of living on the edge (doing everything except "it") has the same effect emotionally and spiritually as having experienced intercourse. I have been stressing the need to maintain *purity* as the ultimate goal for her dating experience.

3. Rather than being put in an emotionally charged situation by being alone with a young man, my daughter is to concentrate on group activities. If there is "safety in a multitude of counselors" then young hormones would do well in the same setting!

4. The "swimsuit" rule is encouraged. Neither the young man nor my daughter is to touch the other's body where a *modest* swimsuit fits. (Of course, this rules out thongs and Speedos!) This very tangible guideline seems to make more sense than just saying they are to refrain from "inappropriate touching." It's a guideline that gives them understandable boundaries.

5. It is important that our family gets to know the young man who is desirous of spending time with our daughter. Therefore, it is imperative that he come and talk with us so we can develop a friendly relationship.

6. It is good to have an age guideline on dating. If the parents are tuned in to their daughter, they should know when she is ready for the responsibility. Some set the age ahead of time, while others rest their decision on how well the daughter is handling other situations such as grades, household chores, church, and civic duties.

7. Provide good books on choosing wisely in the area of dating. Take her to conferences and surround her with positive young people who are being taught the same standards.

8. The "vertical" and "light" rules are helpful. She is to not allow herself the option of being horizontal at any time during the date. For example, do not lie on the floor and watch TV. Sit up straight. Do not lie on her bed and talk to one another. (In fact, there's no need to be in a bedroom at any time.) There seems to be an unseen biological

switch that is tripped when two young, hormonally driven people lie down together. Also keep the lights up. It is amazing how having the lights fully on can bring about good decisions.

9. God has given her the awesome gift of reproduction. However, with it comes an overwhelming responsibility for that privilege. I want my daughter to know, whether right or wrong, the parameters for dating must be set by the woman. Our sense of fairness may lead us to assume that both men and women have equal responsibility in maintaining sexual purity in dating. Before God, of course, that assumption is correct. However, in a very practical sense the girl has more responsibility because she is the "nest" for any potential child that might be conceived. Therefore, her obligation to protect her body and her sense of purity is even more important.

10. The decision for moral purity must be made *before* the date is planned. The ground rules are to be established *before* the agreement to go out. Those who fail to plan to be holy are dangerously planning to fail.

Loving Unconditionally

I want my daughter to understand that she can call me anytime she needs me and tell me anything that is on her heart— knowing that I will love her no matter what. If God who is perfect and holy can love me—a dirty, rotten sinner—in this manner, how can I do less than show the same kind of love to my daughter.

Plan "A" is that she will be smart and heed the instructions given by those who know the rewards and the consequence of actions. Proverbs 4:23-27 warns:

> Watch over your heart with all diligence, for from it flow
> the springs of life. Put away from you a deceitful mouth

and put devious speech far from you. Let your eyes look directly ahead and let your gaze be fixed straight in front of you. Watch the path of your feet and all your ways will be established. Do not turn to the right nor to the left; turn your foot from evil.

In our zeal to shield our daughters from the negatives of wrong choices, we must not turn our backs on them when they fail to do what is right. My friend Betty encountered this situation firsthand.

Betty and I listened to the same teaching tapes on how to be a good mommy, and we attended Bible studies together. Although Betty was a few years older than me and her children were in elementary school while mine were babies and toddlers, I watched with keen interest as she displayed an undying dedication to her children as she home-schooled them and directed them through the tedious and often tempestuous teen years.

When her daughter Sandra turned 18 and was planning to go away to a Christian college, family and friends gathered together to celebrate Sandra's fine character and accomplishments. Her potential to achieve great things was apparent to all who knew her. She was indeed a beautifully talented and obedient daughter.

As it turned out, they sent their daughter off to Bible college only to have her come home for Christmas in her fourth month of pregnancy. It was a sobering lesson in grace and mercy when we all gathered at the church. Now six months pregnant and wearing a white maternity wedding gown, she stood beside a scared, skinny boy who looked far too young to be getting married. His nervous smile revealed the braces still on his teeth.

I'm not sure I passed the "mercy test" with flying colors. I went through the motions, but I was also very unnerved by the possibility that a mother could invest years in teaching all the right things and praying all the right prayers yet still be devastated by the moral choices made on a single evening. Nonetheless, a situation had been put into motion that could not be stopped. Though family and friends made a gallant effort to overlook the obvious nature of the situation, it was quite apparent the consequences of this young couple's decision had a heart-breaking effect.

In my world, I'm more comfortable with absolutes. I want reality to be: If I do this mothering thing right, then my children will make good choices. But many of us have discovered mothering is not an exact science. And mothering formulas do not always work out the way we think they should. Fortunately, we are responsible to do all we know to do, and we can trust God for His care and mercy for all else.

I find it comforting to realize that God did a perfect job parenting Adam and Eve. They didn't have a terrible parent to blame for all their quirks and foibles. No one mistreated them, called them names, or molested their innocent hearts or bodies. Their environment was paradise and every need was met. They only had one thing they were prohibited from doing—eat from the tree of the knowledge of good and evil. With only one restriction placed on them, they still went their own way, disobeying God out of selfish, willful hearts.

If we do all we know to do, we cannot blame ourselves for the bad choices our children make any more than God can be blamed for Adam and Eve's sins.

Mercy and Forgiveness Begin with Us

A mother's merciful and forgiving heart does not begin the moment we offer it to our daughters. It starts as we accept God's unmerited grace toward our own moral lapses and sins.

I have found the most harsh moralists are those who are hiding their own failures. The most gracious and forgiving people are those who understand the frailty of humans because they acknowledge they've failed. When Jesus was rebuffed for letting an immoral woman touch Him as she poured out all she had to anoint His feet, He clearly lavished grace on her. Luke 7:37,38 starts the story. "There was a woman in the city who was a sinner; and when she learned that He was reclining at the table in the Pharisee's house, she brought an alabaster vial of perfume, and standing behind Him at His feet, weeping, she began to wet His feet with her tears, and kept wiping them with the hair of her head, and kissing His feet and anointing them with the perfume."

The Pharisee, a religious leader who kept the law, questioned Jesus' wisdom in letting such an abhorrent person near Him, let alone allowing Himself to be touched by her.

Jesus responded to the Pharisee by telling a story of two debtors. One had debt that totaled a large sum of money, the other was in debt only a few dollars. When it was realized that neither were capable of paying, the money lender forgave both debts. Jesus then asked the question concerning the two: "Which of them will love [the money lender] more?" The answer is the one who has been forgiven the most debt. Later in this chapter Jesus said: "For this reason I say to you, her sins, which are many, have been forgiven, for she loved much; but he who is forgiven little, loves little. And He said to her, 'Your sins have been forgiven'" (verses 47,48).

In our dealings with our daughters, we must first be willing to receive the mercy God has made available for us. He is outrageously forgiving to anyone willing to humble herself and seek forgiveness. He expects us, in turn, to pour out grace on those around us. In James 4:6 we are told that God opposes the proud but gives greater grace to the humble. There are two things evident in this verse: 1) In order to show mercy to my daughter in the face of her stumbling, I must first forsake my pride; and 2) humbly I need to admit my own need for grace.

One mother expressed her deep regret over not making good choices in her moral decisions. She said, "Our daughter has already figured it out that she was born before we were married. We've had to explain what happens when you fail in the area of moral purity. However, I am in the process of building trust with my daughter, and she knows we have repented and that God has forgiven us the sin of allowing our flesh to rule our spirits. She was not a mistake, but we did step out of God's timing. I hope that instead of my past failures serving as an excuse when she is tempted, she will know that God is able to make something good from bad choices. This is a truth I will simply have to allow God to work in her heart."

Helping Your Daughter Get Out of a Bad Situation

What does a young lady do when she realizes she's in a dating relationship in which she is being treated unkindly and with disrespect? For the Christian girl who understands that God regards her as His treasure, staying in this kind of situation is totally unacceptable. Second Timothy 2:21 tells us that each of us can be "a vessel for honor, sanctified, useful to the Master, prepared for every good work." One moment of understanding our immense value to our kind God is worth far more than 1,000 dates with an unkind fellow.

According to Jill Murray, Ph.D., a noted psychotherapist who works in the area of abusive teen relationships, one in three teenage girls will be in a controlling, abusive dating relationship before she graduates from high school. The mistreatment includes verbal and emotional abuse, sexual abuse, and physical battering. Girls who are allowed to date at younger and younger ages are faced with social predicaments they are not mature enough to deal with or have the life experience to handle. They may walk into abusive situations because neither they nor the young men they are dating understand what real love is.

Oftentimes jealous, controlling behavior is mistaken for signs of love. To a girl who craves attention and affection, the unhealthy controlling/manipulative relationship can give a sense of belonging. It isn't until the possessive stranglehold becomes so restrictive she feels she has lost her freedom to choose that she finally becomes dissatisfied. When she begins to resist the attention, the immature boyfriend may become angry and even dangerous.

For instance, I heard a story that involved a 14-year-old girl who was caught in a controlling relationship. She thought she was in love with the boy. Lacking maturity, she was also bereft of the maternal supervision she needed to establish boundaries. The control escalated as the boy began calling 5 to 7 times every night demanding to know her every move. Eventually, the pressure became too much for the young girl. She tried to commit suicide by slitting her wrist. Her boyfriend was also 14. Sadly, this story is repeated far too often.

Excessive jealousy in dating is nothing but a sick form of control. What does God's Word say about the perils of jealousy? James 3:16 warns: "For where jealousy and selfish ambition exist, there is disorder and every evil thing." The next two verses are the flip side: "But the wisdom from above is first *pure, then peaceable, gentle, reasonable, full of mercy and good fruits,* unwavering, without hypocrisy. And the seed whose fruit is righteousness is sown in peace by those who make peace."

Set aside special times when you and your daughter can discuss dating and setting boundaries in private. Help her know that if a dating friendship does not bring the fruit of purity, peacefulness, gentleness, and a sense of good fruit being grown in the life of those dating, then the association should be discontinued. Talk about various ways to do this and be open to listening as she explores her emotional reaction to the situation.

It's also important to equip daughters to deal with dating pressures. Without the help of a mature adult, a teenage girl can become an easy sexual exploit for boys. Often they use the old line, "If you love me, then prove it." I want my daughter to know this is a deception from the pit of hell. If a boy loves her, he would never ask her to do anything that would hurt her, violate her conscience, or hinder her relationship with God. We need to build strong courageous young women willing to stand up for what is right. However, they will only be as moral and courageous as they see demonstrated by their moms or women around them.

Listed below are some of the warning signs of potential problems between boy/girl dating relationships adapted from ideas presented by Dr. Murray in her excellent book *But I Love Him: Protecting Your Teen Daughter from Controlling, Abusive Dating Relationships*. Moms, sit down with your daughter, read this list, and discuss points that pertain to her situation. Daughters, open your hearts, trust your moms, and talk about any of these items that might be of concern to you.

Identifying a Potential Abuser

1. He monopolizes your time.

2. He isolates you from friends and family.

3. He makes you "check-in" with him. He calls a lot.

4. He is extremely jealous or possessive.

5. He says "I love you" early in the relationship.

6. He has an explosive temper. He is aggressive in other areas of his life. Boys who vent their anger by punching holes in the walls or being destructive are dangerous. Eventually their control may slip, leading to assaults or worse. If the boy feels a sense of relief and good feeling after an exploding, this is also not good. Proverbs 22:24 NKJV says, "Make no friendship with an angry man, and with a furious man do not go, lest you learn his ways and

set a snare for your soul." (If you or your daughter is in a dangerous situation, God is directing you through His Word to make a change.)

7. He puts his hands on you in a hurtful way and calls it playing. Roughhousing is not acceptable behavior between a boy and girl. It could easily turn into rougher play than anticipated and someone may get hurt. If it doesn't feel right to you, then be assured that it's not.

8. He doesn't take responsibility for his own actions and reactions. He blames you for bringing out the worse in him. He says things like, "It's all your fault" and "You made me do it." He seems to have a dual personality—one minute being nice, the next being aggressive.

9. He wants to control what you wear.

10. He calls you names and embarrasses you in front of others.

11. He has a history of abuse in his family.

12. He uses drugs and alcohol.

13. You feel the need to rescue him from situations.[4]

God sees us as individuals of immense value. If we conduct ourselves in a dignified manner and show that same attitude to others, we will reap incredible rewards. The following lyrics were written to encourage single men and women.

The Treasure

Girl, don't give his treasure away.
It's for a man somewhere in time who is willing to wait
'Til the day, he can call you by his name.
Girl, don't give his treasure away.

But if you've done it, and you wonder what you should do
Just remember, go to Jesus and He will make you brand-new.
And when He restores your treasure to its original state,
Until the right time
Don't give it away.

Young man, I know it's very hard to see.
That just beyond the way you feel is the man you want to be.
So keep it pure for that woman who waits.
Boy, don't give her treasure away.

But if you've done it, and you wonder what you should do
Just remember, go to Jesus and He will make you brand-new.
And when He restores your treasure to its original state,
Until the right time don't give it away.
Until the right time, don't give it away.[5]

4

Marvels of Marriage

I want my daughter to know that being
a wife to a godly man is the highest honor
and calling she could experience.
As a helpmate, she is part of
a God-ordained team.

A Good Wife

The marriage of my daughter was a glorious event. Together we had thought about, planned for, and saved up for this day for more than a year. Steve and I willingly invested an unforgettable amount of money in the event. Why? Because we viewed the great value of our daughter, and presenting her to our son-in-law deserved our best effort. He was not just getting a wife; Emmitt Beall was receiving a picture of a truth found in Genesis 2. In the passage it is recorded that Adam, the first man, was enjoying a perfect, sinless relationship with God. Every need was met and he was literally living in paradise. God looked at him, however, and declared, "Something is not right." Actually, God said in verse 18: "It is not good for the man to be alone; I will make him a helper suitable for him." And what was God's solution to the man's problem?

Enter the woman. With Eve in his life, Adam was complete.

The New Testament carries this same message of importance as it pertains to a woman's relationship with a man. First Corinthians 11:9,12 states: "For indeed man was not created for the woman's sake, but woman for the man's sake....For as the woman originates from the man, so also the man has his birth through the woman; and all things originate from God." From the beginning it was God's divine plan that man and woman work together in marriage to accomplish His purpose. The wife has a significant role to play that must not be diminished.

I want my daughter to understand the importance of her part in this arrangement. The last few months Heidi was living at home before she got married, we walked each evening. For three miles each day, we talked and explored the ideas of home and family. Among those discussions were in-depth conversations about how she could contribute to the "Beall team." I stressed that being husband and wife is simply *taking care of one another* in every area of life.

I Want My Daughter to Know the Basic Marriage Principles

Countless books have been written on the subject of marriage (including *Married Lovers, Married Friends* by Steve and me). But I pray that the following discussion may be a way you and your daughter can explore what God intended for the wife in this special, God-ordained relationship. To explore the diverse dimensions of marriage, here's an acrostic.

Model the life of Christ before your husband

Adorn yourself

Rule over your tongue

Respect and admiration are essential

Include him in your prayers

Accept your differences and make them work for you

Grant him the place of headship in your family

Engage physically with joy, enthusiasm, and frequency

Model the Life of Christ Before Your Husband

On rare occasions Steve has accompanied me on a shopping trip to the mall. When he does, it's exciting to try on dresses and walk out to get his reaction. When he really likes an outfit, I am likely to take it home (if it is reasonable in cost). If he offers a tentative "hmmm," I move on to something else.

Modeling dresses for my man can be a risky undertaking. Because I want him to be honest, I have to be willing to hear remarks I may not want to receive. One comment is particularly memorable. I exited the fitting room, pulled the entry curtain back, and did my runway spin. Steve leaned back in his chair and said, "Too young for you!"

Ouch! I set out to find one of those "old" dresses, and soon Steve discovered that "old" dresses can cost a lot more than "young" ones.

While clothes modeling for a husband can sometimes leave a wife feeling as though she looks like a bag lady, there is one garment she can don that will cause her to always be radiantly beautiful. That garment is Christ.

By "putting on" the robe of the righteousness of Christ, a woman is transformed from ordinary to extraordinary. His demeanor becomes hers. His attitude of service sparkles within her. Philippians 2:3,4 encourages us to "do nothing from selfishness or empty conceit, but with humility of mind regard one another as more important than yourselves; do not merely look out for your own personal interests, but also for the interest of others." Not only does a woman's outlook create a mysterious beauty a godly man will appreciate, but even a man who may not care for the things of the Lord can be "won over" when a woman drapes her life in Christ. A wonderful example of this is found in my mother-in-law, Lillian Chapman. The following is her story.

Winning Without a Word

They met in the honky-tonks of Logan County, West Virginia. The jitterbug was their dance of choice, and their favorite drink was a strong one. Feeling the fire of young love, they dated and soon married. She was 18; he was 20.

Setting up their home in the small town was no problem since they were surrounded by family and close friends. They easily settled into life. He worked days, and she attended college in the evenings while he watched their two small children. They still partied on occasion, drinking and smoking and hanging out with friends.

One night, on her way to a night class, Lillian walked by a church and heard music coming from inside. She knew if she went into the church she would be late for school, but there was an undeniable pull, a tug on her heart to check it out. What was it about this simple church and the energetic music that held her attention?

She slipped through the back door, sat down, and was never the same. That night during a revival meeting she made the great exchange. She gave Jesus her broken spirit, her sinful heart, and her aimless wanderings. In return, He gave her a brand-new life filled with peace and purpose.

When she returned to their little home that night, her husband, P.J., enquired as to how her class had been. She told him the truth. There had been a change; she was hanging up her book bag and going to church.

And go to church she did. Whenever the doors were open, she was sitting with her children, drinking it all in. She didn't have to tell her husband things were different. He could see it. He saw that his wife, the chain-smoker, no longer desired cigarettes. He noticed she spent her time reading her Bible and praying. That which once made her angry and spiteful now drove her into the bedroom and down on her knees. He could tell when she came out of her "prayer closet" that something had happened inside her. There was no denying it. She was different.

It didn't take long before P.J. decided to check out what was going on down at the little church. He went with her to help with the children, but he was the one who got helped. Within six months he gloriously chose Jesus.

The habits that had gripped them were now choices they laid aside. No one had to tell them to stop drinking and change their behavior. Their tastes had changed. They no longer desired the things that once held their attention.

How does Scripture tell us we can win an unbelieving, non-Christian spouse? Certainly not by nagging! True conversion is not accomplished by leaving Bible verses around the house or even by getting the pastor to come and talk to a mate. The actions and attitudes that adorn the message of a life that has been changed make faith appealing. Christians are called to be the salt of the earth. Salt creates a thirst, and only the Living Water of Christ can quench that craving. If we could talk our spouses into the kingdom, we'd all give it a whirl. But we can't. God must draw them. John 6:44 says: "No one can come to Me unless the Father who sent Me draws him."

We must also demonstrate our faith and hope in Christ before their eyes. Obviously it can be done. In fact, generations of Chapmans will be grateful for the transforming power my mother-in-law allowed to be worked in her life. And it all started when a young wife let God change her, then stepped back and let God work on her husband.

It is my hope that as I modeled Christ to the best of my ability, Heidi will do the same if she has a daughter. I want my daughter to know one reason I could model Christ was because my mother did so before me. The following lyrics were written by Steve to highlight my mom's diligence to "act like Jesus."

Watching You

Early mornings in the kitchen
Smell of coffee in the air
Sent out like an invitation
For your man to join you there

I could hear your conversation
Tho I could not hear the words
But from my bedroom down the hallway
Two hearts in love is what I heard

Before he'd leave to make a living
You'd whisper something in his ear

Then he'd smile and look around the room
As if he hoped no one could hear

While he was gone you were faithful
I never saw you waste your time
You did him right by his labor
I never saw you waste a dime

These are the thoughts I had this morning
As the smell of coffee filled the air
And a man as sweet as my daddy
Came in the room to join me there

Mom, I'll be forever grateful
For the lessons that I saw
'Cause there's a girl that might be listening
From her bedroom down the hall

And the way you loved my daddy
Was the best thing you could do
To teach a young girl how to love a man
I learned it all from watching you[6]

Adorn Yourself

While the mysteriously majestic robe of Christ will please the spiritual eyes of a man, it is important to remember that men also have eyes of flesh. For that reason, whether we like it not, we must admit that men are visual. They are stimulated and aroused by what they see. I want my daughter to know she has a God-given responsibility to her husband to maintain a lovely physical appearance along with her spiritual appearance. It can be easy for some Christian women to forget their outward look. To keep a good balance, a woman should not ignore 1 Samuel 16:7: "For God sees not as man sees, for man looks at the outward appearance, but the LORD looks at the heart."

Being attentive to our looks is even implied in some traditional wedding ceremonies when the bride and groom promise to "keep oneself" for the other. In years past when I heard that phrase, I thought it meant to make sure the marriage partners were sexually exclusive to each other. And I'm sure this is an intended part of the pledge. However, that promise goes beyond the maintenance of marital fidelity. We have an obligation to "keep" ourselves attractive to our spouses.

Some women expect their husbands to look at them with "Superman" eyes. Husbands are asked to look past the outside and see only who the wives are inside. Eventually, husbands may do that; however, it is our responsibility as wives to make that journey as painless as possible. I am not saying that when we signed the marriage certificates we were, in essence, signing a contract assuring our spouses we would remain the same size and shape for 25 years. Our spouses cannot expect that of us any more than we can require them to maintain their same waist measurement and have the same head of hair they had when we married. There are some changes that inevitably take place over time and are beyond our control. Nevertheless, I do believe there is an implied obligation to bring our very best to the marriage—regardless of our ages. "Best" doesn't mean perfection, but it does suggest we are to offer our finest physical self to our mates. This includes maintaining good hygiene, dressing neatly, and keeping up a respectful appearance.

In his book *His Needs, Her Needs,* Willard Harley tells about a couple who came in for counseling. They had been married for five years when they came to see him. Their marriage was in bad shape and...and so was Nancy. Before Nancy met Harold, she was in her late 20s and about 80 pounds overweight. She longed to get married and have a family, but she seldom dated. Men seemed to not be attracted to her physically, so she decided to make some changes in order to accomplish her goal of finding a husband. Nancy enrolled in an exercise class, cut back on her calorie intake, and shed the excess pounds.

She bought a new wardrobe to show off her great figure, fixed her hair, and was ready for whatever came next. Nancy was a knockout, and the men responded favorably by calling for dates. She met Harold, hit it off, and within eight months they were married.

The first thing Nancy did after marrying Harold was to quit her job. She stayed home and immediately began to regain the weight she had lost. By the time this couple came to see Dr. Harley, their marriage was in jeopardy. Nancy was hurt because she wanted Harold to love her for who she was inside. Harold was upset because he had married someone who was physically appealing, and he had assumed she would stay that way.

Dr. Harley writes, "Granted, some men do not care about physical appearance. Their wives can be overweight or underweight; it makes no difference. They have other emotional needs that are far more important than the need for an attractive spouse. But Nancy had not married one of these men. In fact, she had married a man for whom physical appearance was at the top of his list. He needed an attractive wife."[7]

Harold and Nancy's story is a sobering reminder that keeping our promise to bring our very best to the marriage is not a pledge to take lightly.

Rule over Your Tongue

On October 8, 1871, the great Chicago fire started. It was reported that 17,500 buildings were destroyed, 300 people died, and 125,000 others were left homeless. What caused such a catastrophe? Was the fire started by the aftermath of a blazing meteor collision? Was it the act of a terrorist or an attack by a foreign enemy? No, legend has it that Mrs. O'Leary was simply milking her cow when the rowdy bovine kicked over the lantern that ignited the barn. And the rest is history.

In James 3 we read of another kind of "small" beginning that can set a fire and unleash destruction. That blazemaker is located between our noses and chins. You guessed it—the tongue. That fleshy member is not only called a *fire out of control,* capable of destroying our homes and lives, but it is also labeled an *unbridled horse,* a *rudderless ship,* an *untamed wild animal,* and a *venomous poison.*

I want my daughter to know that her words will either bring harm or harmony to her marriage. It's her responsibility to control the words *she says* and *how she says them.* Her attitude, which will be reflected in her conversation, greatly impacts the kind of place her home will be and whether her family will feel safe and loved. With such potential for harm, we must make sure we rule over our tongues in every area of our lives, especially in our relationships with our husbands. When it comes to our marriages, an unruly, misdirected tongue can burn down the very spirits of those we love and leave their hearts in a pile of ashes.

One day I was talking to a good friend and a fine Christian woman. She was relating to me the mean-spirited words she had said during a disagreement with her husband. His hurt response to her cutting remarks branded into my heart. He said, "You can castrate a man with your tongue faster than someone could with a knife." As wives we indeed have the power of life and death in our tongues (Proverbs 18:21). What can we do to control the words we say?

First of all, we must see the necessity of disciplining our talk. James 1:19,20 says: "This you know, my beloved brethren. But everyone must be quick to hear, slow to speak and slow to anger; for the anger of man does not achieve the righteousness of God." He goes on to say in verse 26: "If anyone thinks himself to be religious, and yet does not bridle his tongue but deceives his own heart, this man's religion is worthless."

We are like tubes of toothpaste. When we are under pressure and "squeezed" by life, what's inside of us will come out. No one else is responsible for our sharp, hurting remarks. We all get irritated with family and friends from time to time, but if we express that frustration with poisonous words *we* are the ones to blame for the escalation of the problem. If, on the other hand, the words we express are filled with mercy, grace, and forgiveness, then we know we have filled our hearts and minds with good things. The Word of God will be evident in our lives if that is what we have been ingesting.[8]

The words may come out across our tongues, but the problem originates in the heart. Matthew 12:34 NKJV: "For out of the abundance of the heart the mouth speaks." If we seek to rule over our words, then we do that by making sure what is in us is something worthy of being heard and said. First Peter 3:10-12 says:

> The one who desires life, to love and see good days, must keep his tongue from evil and his lips from speaking deceit. He must turn away from evil and do good; he must seek peace and pursue it. For the eyes of the Lord are toward the righteous, and His ears attend to their prayers, but the face of the Lord is against those who do evil.

Respect and Admiration Are Essential

I want my daughter to know she needs to show her husband that she loves him *and* respects him. It's crucial that she assures him of her admiration for who he is and what God has planned for him.

God commands the husband to *love his wife* even as himself, and the woman is to *respect her husband*. Perhaps God is addressing our natural tendency to serve self. Is the man so inclined to wrap his life around his work and his own needs that it's easy for him to neglect one of the basic necessities for a woman—to receive love and affection? And is God compelled to remind the woman to step beyond her propensity to criticize and correct instead of meeting one of the fundamental requirements of a man? Does the Lord want him to be admired for his work *and* for who he is? It seems so.

There are at least three areas where a husband needs respect and admiration: his ability to perform, to provide, and to protect. A wise wife will encourage her husband in these areas. While understanding her contribution, she will also be aware of her incredible influence on his development of character...like the woman in the following story.

> One day the mayor of a town was walking along the street with his wife at his side. He looked over to a building site where construction was under way. He eyed a man his wife had once dated. The mayor said, "Look! There's your old boyfriend. Just think, if you had married him you would be the wife of a construction worker." His wife didn't even glance toward the workers. She confidently said, "No, dear, if I had married him, he'd be the mayor."

The old adage, "Behind every good man is a great woman" is true in many ways. As wives, we have a great deal to do with whether or not our mates will be all they can be.

One way of showing respect for your husband is to express it verbally. Proverbs 31:26 NKJV says: "She opens her mouth with wisdom, and on her tongue is the law of kindness." Expressing words of encouragement to your husband is like giving him a cool glass of water on a hot, muggy day or, as Proverbs 25:11 NKJV states: "A word fitly spoken is like apples of gold in settings of silver."

Don't be stingy with those words of praise for your spouse. Speak well of him in front of your children, extended family members, and friends. Let all who know you see and hear the respect you have for your husband. Good words are contagious. Others will see him in a positive light if you do.

There are opportunities, not only for good words but also for actions. There's a legend told concerning a knight who was taken captive by the Moslem Saladin during the Crusades:

The knight begged for his life to be spared, claiming he had a wife in England who loved him very much. Saladin commented that the wife would soon forget him and marry another. The equestrian warrior insisted that his wife was fully devoted to him and loved him beyond measure. The chieftain decided to see if what the knight said was true. Saladin offered to set the young man free if his wife would send her right hand as a token of love for her husband.

When word arrived to the wife, she immediately cut off her right hand and sent it to the commander. The nobleman was then released to return home to her.

Gratefully, God has not asked us to sacrifice our hands to show our love, but He has asked us to give our *hearts* to our husbands. Showing respect and honor may be difficult for some women because they have married a man who is, to be quite frank, a dishonorable person in many of his attitudes, actions, and accomplishments. In times when our life experiences seem to be at odds with the Word of God we have to make a choice— obedience or rebellion. When we choose to obey God rather than what seems right in our own eyes, God will intervene on our behalf (see Proverbs 3:5-8). When we obey God's Word, submitting to Christ and respecting our husbands, we are not saying, "My husband is such a perfect man, I cannot help but respect him." We are simply accepting the men we have chosen for our mates as instruments of God's refining work in our lives. In those difficult times we are to love and respect our husbands. However, we are to *put our trust in God* and His promise to work all things together for our good (see Romans 8:28).

I very much respect and admire the husband God has given me. I could have never been clever enough to pick Steve on my own. Without question, it was a divine act of grace. There is no doubt in my mind that God brought us together; therefore, I stand humble and grateful for a gift I did not deserve. On the occasion of our twenty-fifth anniversary I had the privilege of expressing those feelings of love and respect in a letter. Steve has given me permission to share the letter with you.

March 29, 2000

Dear Steve,

It's hard to believe that twenty-five years have come and gone since we stood in that little Methodist church and made forever promises. The vows I pledged that day were words I didn't fully comprehend, but I meant them...and I still do.

Living with you has been the easiest thing I've ever done. You are a joy to work with, and I am blessed each morning as you grace my life with your kindness and gentle ways. You not only meet my every need but you fully feed and satisfy my soul.

The passionate hunger which burned during our courtship and early years of marriage has become an eternal flame whose glowing embers ignite at the very thought or sight of you. Our love's intense quality could only be compared to what time does to transform grape juice to a fine vintage wine. I am intoxicated with your love. I can never get my fill.

You are all and more than I ever dreamed of in a man. But well beyond the marital relationship grows a deep and abiding respect and admiration for you as a talented, thoroughly attractive, godly example of the most interesting and completely fascinating human person I've been privileged to encounter.

I am honored to have shared your life, your children, your work, and your bed these many years. My only request is to have at least twenty-five more.

I am completely devoted....

...Annie

Include Him in Your Prayers

I want my daughter to know she has a spiritual obligation and opportunity to support her spouse in prayer.

Steve had complained of a tightness in his neck, but we thought it was just the residue of a bad cold he'd had a couple of weeks before. To make sure it was nothing, we decided it would be best if a physician were consulted. Steve got ready and together we went to see the doctor. As the physician probed and pressed at his swollen glands on the side of his neck, we expected to hear the reassuring words, "Oh, that's nothing. I see this all the time." Instead, the doctor said with a pained look on his face, "Oh my! Does that hurt?"

Steve was sent home with some antibiotics and an appointment to come back later that week for more tests. The night before the biopsy which would determine whether this condition was serious or silly, we lay in our bed staring at the ceiling. Steve finally spoke. "I was really hoping to get to see the children raised." He then turned over and went to sleep. For me, sleep was out of the question. This was a night spent crying out to the Lord for help and healing.

It is at those times of supreme crisis that we can clearly see our need for God to intervene. In this particular situation we made our request through united prayer to God and graciously He answered (see Matthew 18:19). Steve was fine. However, those times of trouble are defining moments that remind us of our total dependence on God's help and mercy.

As wives we have the privilege of wielding the weapon of prayer against the enemy of our marriages. God has promised that when we call to Him, He will hear our petitions and answer. Matthew 7:7-11 are wonderful verses to claim over our husbands as we pray for them:

> Ask, and it will be given to you; seek, and you will find;
> knock, and it will be opened to you. For everyone who

asks receives, and he who seeks finds, and to him who knocks it will be opened. Or what man is there among you who, when his son asks for a loaf, will give him a stone? Or if he asks for a fish, he will not give him a snake, will he? If you then, being evil, know how to give good gifts to your children, how much more will your Father who is in heaven give what is good to those who ask Him!

Seeking to be the kind of helpmate God has called me to be I have created the H-E-L-P method of praying for my husband. Perhaps this will help you pray for your mate.

Pray for his head, endeavors, love for God and others, and physical health. Praying for his *head:* that his thoughts, will and emotions will be controlled by, and line up with, the Word of God. His *endeavors:* that he will prosper and find purpose for that which God has called him to accomplish. His *love:* that his love for the Lord and others will grow and become stronger. His *physical* health: that his body, which is the temple of the Holy Spirit, will be healthy, able, and free from disease.

Here are a few passages from the Bible to help you pray according to the will of God on these issues. As you find additional Scriptures that help you in your prayers, add them to the list.

Head	Endeavors	Love	Physical Health
Mark 12:30	Proverbs 16:3	Psalm 20:4;	Jeremiah 30:17
Romans 7:23	Ecclesiastes 5:19	139:23,24	Isaiah 40:31
Philippians	Colossians 3:17,23	Proverbs 3:1-3	2 Corinthians
3:7,8;4:6,7	2 Thessalonians	1 Peter 3:15	4:16
	1:11		3 John 2

I recommend that you set a particular weekday for praying for your mate. Perhaps this prayer/song adaptation will further assist you in praying for your husband:

Wednesday's Prayer

Father God, to you I come in the name of Your Son.
I bring my husband to Your throne; Father, hear my prayer
Above all else, Lord, save his soul.
Draw him near You, keep him close
Be the shield against his foes; make him Yours, not mine

Guide his feet, Lord, light his path. May his eyes on You be cast
And give his hands a kingdom task, a purpose for his years.
Give him peace in Christ alone. And in his sorrow, be his song
No other joy will last as long, Father, calm his fears

And as my flesh cries out for bread, may I hunger, Lord, instead
That my husband would be fed on Your Words of life
So, Father God, to You I come in the name of Your Son
I bring my husband to Your throne; Father hear my prayer.[9]

Accept Your Differences

I want my daughter to know that in acknowledging that she and her husband are different, she will find strength to make her marriage and life better.

When you talk to people who are newly engaged or just married one of the first things they tell you is all they have in common: They both like the same foods, the same music, and they like to go to the same places. You'd think they were identical twins instead of a couple in love. However, it doesn't take them long to figure out they are not as much alike as they thought they were. So what happened? How could two people change in such a short time? The truth be told, no one changed. The whole dating experience teaches them to try to be what the other person wants, rather than revealing to them who they really are. Consequently, there is a degree of disappointment that takes place when faced with the fact that they married someone so different from their expectations. What is the answer to this dilemma? My suggestion is deal with it! It isn't so bad being different from one another!

Steve and I decided a long time ago not to let our disagreements become wedges that would eventually drive us apart and cause us to despise one another. We purposed to appreciate the fact we are different. Differences do to relationships what spices do to chili. They make it better. Spices keep the chili from being bland; differences keep our relationship from being boring. Through the years we've learned to appreciate each other and laugh about the things that make us so diverse (and could potentially drive us nutty). Here's a song we wrote that expresses *some* of our challenges. They may sound familiar.

Incompatibility

Steve: I like a little mayo
Annie: Mustard is my thing

Steve: Make my bread as white as cotton
Annie: I'll have wheat with seven grains

Annie: And a little candle glowing when we eat is what I like
Steve: I need to see what I'm consuming, so please turn on the lights

Annie: I go to bed before the news
Steve: I'm still awake at two A.M.

Annie: I'm up before the chicken
Steve: If I can, I'm sleeping in

Steve: I like wearing huntin' clothes
Annie: I like huntin' clothes to wear

Annie: I'll always ask directions
Steve: I'll find my own way there

Annie: I like a walk in the park
Steve: And I would rather run

Steve: How far can we go on empty
Annie: I've never seen that as fun

Steve: I like talking to my buddies when we're teeing off at ten
Annie: My greens and conversation are a salad bar with friends

Annie: My feet are like December
Steve: And mine are like July

Annie: While I'm piling on the blankets
Steve: I lay there and fry

Annie: I married Ebenezer Scrooge
Steve: I married Mrs. Claus

Annie: While I'm watching *Casablanca*
Steve: I'd rather be watching football

Together: We've got incompatibility everywhere we turn
But still we stay together 'cause there's a lesson we have learned
That if this man and woman were in every way the same
One of us would not be needed, and wouldn't that be a shame[10]

Grant Him Headship

I want my daughter to know she is to honor her husband as the God-ordained head of the family. First Peter 3:1 states: "In the same way, you wives, be submissive to your own husbands."

As a young woman I found this particular tenant of a Christian marriage hard to swallow. The very thought that a wife was to dutifully obey the whims of her husband was inconceivable. During my limited life experience I had observed enough marriages to understand the majority of the husbands I knew were not only unworthy of submission, but they were far too incompetent to run things alone.

One of the contributing factors to this attitude had to do with growing up in the 50s and 60s. During that time I was influenced by the feminist movement of the day. Even though I had surrendered my life to Christ by my late teen years, I came away from that era with a great disdain and hatred for men and children. It would take a divine work in my heart through the transforming power of the Word of God for me to come to understand the *true* biblical meaning of submission as it pertained to the marriage union.

Part of my abhorrence to the idea was rooted in a basic misunderstanding and ignorance of the purpose and meaning of this doctrine. There is a biblical mandate for *all believers to submit to one another*. We are to voluntarily put ourselves under authority (see Ephesians 5:21). This concept has nothing to do with being coerced, enslaved, or lorded over by force. Neither does biblical submission have anything to do with superiority versus inferiority. It does, however, have everything to do with a divine order.

Without question there is an order delegated to the family system. Ephesians 5:22-24 teaches: "Wives, be subject to your own husbands, as to the Lord. For the husband is the head of the wife, as Christ also is the head of the church, He Himself being the Savior of the body. But as the church is subject to Christ, so also the wives ought to be to their husbands in everything." This is an emotionally charged statement to many women. Let's look at a couple of truths in this text that are often misunderstood.

First, the words "be subject" do not mean "obey." They are two *totally different* words in the Greek language. The wife is not expected to obey her husband like a child obeys his parents or an employee obeys an employer. She is to *voluntarily relinquish* her independent rights.

Second, the phrase "your own husbands" suggests an intimate, mutually exclusive relationship. During my man-hating years, I thought the Bible commanded all women to obey all men. Thankfully, that is not the case.

Considering the scriptural mandate for a wife to subject herself to her own husband, it behooves a woman to be careful and marry a man worthy of that commitment. A smart woman will take a good, long look at the man she's interested in and ask some serious questions: Does he have the character of God exuding from his life? Does his demeanor display humility, love, and a mutually submissive attitude? Does he love God and hate sin? If the answer to any of these questions is no, then turn around and run...run fast...and go far!

In the Song of Solomon God has provided a beautiful example for marriage. Although the husband in this narrative was a king and accustomed to being revered and obeyed, the marriage in this book is not maintained by heavy-handed authority; instead it's an attentive, passionate love relationship. There is not even a hint of the husband lording over the wife.

In chapter 2:3,4 we read from the heart of the wife:

> Like an apple tree among the trees of the forest, so is my beloved among the young men. In his shade I took great delight and sat down, and his fruit was sweet to my taste. He has brought me to his banquet hall, and his banner over me is love.

How befitting. In Solomon's day a banner was a public announcement of loyalty. By displaying a banner, the king wanted everyone to know how much he loved his wife.

The husband responded by saying of his bride:

> Arise, my darling, my beautiful one, and come along!...Let me see your form, let me hear your voice; for your voice is sweet, and your form is lovely (2:13,14).

Engage Physically with Joy, Enthusiasm, and Frequency

I want my daughter to know she has the privilege of meeting her husband's sexual needs.

If I were to address the subject of marriage and fail to encourage (i.e., train, instruct, show by example) a young wife in the area of physically expressing love to her husband, I would have failed miserably. A very important aspect of marriage is the participating in and the enjoyment of the marital union.

I once heard it said that when the sexual relationship is good between a husband and wife, it is regarded as only 10 percent important. However, when it's not going well, its importance climbs to 90 percent. We have the wonderful opportunity to not only please and serve God, but to also show that self-giving love to our spouses in the form of physical affection and sexual satisfaction. As wives, we are the only ones in the entire universe who have the God-given right of meeting those special needs. Absolutely no other human is allowed to touch our husbands in the way we can. And no one else is free to offer the words of love and arousal we are allowed to say.

Before we read what God has to say concerning our responsibility to love and fulfill our spouses' sexual needs, let us first consider Proverbs 14:1: "The wise woman builds her house, but the foolish tears it down [utterly ruins] with her own hands." When we constantly choose work, activities, other people, and even our own self-interest over the needs of our spouses, we are literally destroying our homes. It doesn't take many incidences of rejecting our husbands' sexual advances before they get the idea that their needs are not important to us.

Unless we are committed to a limited time of prayer and fasting, have an illness, or are logistically separated from our spouses, we should make our sexual relationships a priority. First Corinthians 7:5 admonishes us to "stop depriving one another, except by agreement for a time, so that you may devote yourself to prayer, and come together again so that Satan will not tempt you because of your lack of self-control." Proverbs 5:15-19 also instructs us in this area of our marriage:

> Drink water from your own cistern and fresh water from your own well. Should your springs be dispersed abroad, streams of water in the streets? Let them be yours alone and not for strangers with you. Let your fountain be blessed, and rejoice in the wife of your youth. As a loving hind and a graceful doe, let her breasts satisfy you at all times; be exhilarated always with her love.

Steve and I addressed this important topic in these lyrics:

Cup Filled Up with Love

Something happens when a pretty young girl
Smiles at a married man
It'll take him back for a moment
Then he'll wonder just where he stands
And if his cup of love is empty 'cause he can't drink at home
When another woman offers her drink
Temptation comes on strong

Now a woman can see when there's lust in the eyes
Of a man who is looking her way
And even though she's married there's something exciting
In the kind words a stranger might say
And if her cup of love is empty 'cause she can't drink at home
When another man offers his drink
Temptation comes on strong

You've got to keep his cup
Filled up with love
And don't ever let it run dry
Keep him drinking at home and when he's out there alone
It'll help him let temptation go on by[11]

Anyone who thinks God is a prude obviously has never read the Bible! The sexual relationship is encouraged, blessed, and commanded—but only within the bonds of marriage. As a wife willingly and lovingly meets the needs of her husband, she is pleasing her spouse and obeying God's instruction.

We have been warned through the direction of the Scriptures and we are left to decide whether we will embrace God's admonition, or be like the foolish woman and pay the price with a home in ruin.

5

True Motherhood

I want my daughter to know that
there is no job, career, office, position,
or opportunity that remotely compares
to the importance of being a mother.

Until You Have One of Your Own...

A holiday gathering is always a lot of fun for my family. Since my five siblings live scattered across the country it's a special occasion when we make the supreme effort to get together. I don't know how the rest of the world does it, but for our West Virginia family, the men and women gather in the dining room to eat the meal. And what a meal it is. With the table weighted down with foods of every kind, our dinner makes the first Thanksgiving look like a child's Happy Meal from McDonald's. After the feast is over the men move to another room to watch football games and the women stay at the table. (It's after the men leave, by the way, that we do our serious eating. Yep! We undo the top button on our pants and just...keep eating. Oh, the joys of life!)

Since all of us only manage to get together once a year it's a great time to catch up with what is going on in each family. My niece was obviously expecting a baby in the spring. So I innocently posed a simple question. "After your baby is born, are you going to get to stay home to raise it?"

I noticed when I made the inquiry that she flinched a tad. She then squared her shoulders, looked me straight in the eye, and said something quite troubling: "I would hate to think I would limit my life by staying home with a baby. That's what daycare centers are for."

Keeping in mind this was a family function and I didn't want to cause a problem, I didn't say anything...for a minute. But I was compelled to respond because my heart was broken. Her statement was so disappointing because I realized she was the voice of my daughter's generation.

Where did this lovely young woman learn she could do anything with her life that was more important than raising her own baby? She didn't learn it from my mother's generation. No, unfortunately, she learned it from mine. My heart ached as I realized what an injustice my generation has done to the young women who are just starting their families.

Today's mothers have been told they can pay someone to feed their babies, pay for someone to diaper them, and pay to keep them occupied. But there is a truth that has been withheld from them: Love cannot be bought. The very best daycare providers still cannot truly love and care as much as a parent can. Their most valiant effort is not the same and, by all means, not enough.

In recent years our country has experienced an epidemic of teen violence. The school shootings and the general mayhem we have seen on the news should cause us to question what has happened in our nation. When referring to the misguided and sometimes violent teenagers I've heard people say, "Those children act like animals." If that be the case, then the question to raise is: "If they act like animals, could it be because they have been raised in herds?" In God's original plan it was never intended for children to be raised in groups and by nonfamily members.

John 10:11-13 says:

> I am the good shepherd; the good shepherd lays down his life for the sheep. He who is a hired hand, and not a shepherd, who is not the owner of the sheep, sees the wolf coming, and leaves the sheep and flees, and the wolf snatches them and scatters them. He flees because he is a hired hand and not concerned about the sheep.

If this passage is applied to parenting, it yields a sobering truth. When we look around at the children who seem so without hope and direction, it appears that the lack of parental involvement and protection has given the "wolf," the enemy of our souls, the opportunity to snatch our "sheep" out from under our noses. We need the next generation of women to not only forgive us but also to correct the tragic mistake of forfeiting the divine responsibility of raising our own babies.

A Change of Heart; A Change of Vision

I have not always felt so protective toward children. When I was growing up, being a mother was nowhere on my list of "want tos." I never babysat or had any desire to be around kids. Basically, I saw children as a messy nuisance that would eat up my time, energy, and resources. It was with this selfish attitude firmly intact that Steve and I got married. Before we tied the knot, we discussed my lack of desire to have kids. Since it didn't seem important to Steve at the time, we proceeded with our marriage with the issue of children settled. There would be none.

Well, perhaps that's not exactly an accurate assessment of our understanding. I determined we wouldn't have children, and I thought Steve agreed with me. After we'd been married a little while I reminded him of our discussion and subsequent understanding. Upon considering the subject, he sincerely and innocently asserted that he had no recollection of that conversation. He pleaded insanity and I believed him. A few months later we attended a Bill Gothard Institute in Basic Youth Conflicts Seminar. During one of the sessions the matter of having offspring was covered. As it turned out, Steve received a revelation and I got pregnant!

As I reflect on those antichild attitudes I fostered for so many years, I am reminded of a country song recorded by the popular singer, Garth Brooks, entitled "Thank God for Unanswered Prayers." My aversion and determination to not have children is one of those "unanswered prayers" for which I am most grateful. Our children have been a joy beyond description. And the addition of a son-in-law, daughter-in-law, and grandchildren have added to our delight.

Motherhood Is Lending Our Wombs

Without question, good mommies give of themselves to their children. The first thing we do is offer them our bodies as a temporary shelter. As we house, nourish, protect, and carry them around the first nine months of their existence, it is but a preview of how much they will own our hearts and minds in the years to come. Adoptive moms also carry and labor on behalf of their children. Some mothers have told me that the duration of their travail was not for hours or even days, but some women literally labored in prayer for years for children. The following lyrics were written to acknowledge the sacrificial love adoptive parents offer to their children.

Labor of My Heart

I would have given anything
To be the one to know the pain
Of bringing you into this world, but it couldn't be

Though I did not bring you here
Still I labored in my tears
Through the long nights I prayed
You would come to me

You are the labor of my heart
Child, you are the labor of my heart
With all my strength I prayed, till they laid you in my arms
Child, you are the labor of my heart

Blessed be the maker of bone, of other bone
He made flesh of my desire
And now we take you home[12]

Whether we have borne or gathered children to us, we are held captive by these little ones. My grandmother, Naomi, who was the mother of six children said it well: "From the moment we know we're expecting a child, they dominate our every thought. We love them and worry about them until the day we die. If they, God forbid, would die first, we then grieve ourselves to death over them."

I didn't understand the truth of grandma's statement until I had my own beautiful children. It was only then that I felt that mother/child connection Grandma was talking about. Now I cannot conceive of what life would have been without them.

If I had been better acquainted with the Word of God, I might have been more open to the biblical attitude concerning child-bearing. It wasn't until I was expecting our first child that I came across this passage in 1 Timothy 2:15 that served to bring a divine calm to my anxious heart: "But women will be preserved [healed, set free, rescued] through the bearing of children if they continue in faith and love and sanctity with self-restraint."

Motherhood Is Sharing Our Wisdom

I want to offer my daughter basic ideas she can use to build her own strategy for raising children. It would be beyond arrogant of me to presume to tell her how to raise her child. As many of us have already surmised, mothering is not an exact science and no two children are the same.

Doing the work of a mom is one of those professions that requires continual "on the job training" because it's a position in a constant state of mutation. Just about the time moms get the hang of it, the rules are changed. For instance, I was scared to death to take care of an infant. I was sure I would do something wrong, and the child would die. Even worse, I had nightmares I would forget where I put the baby!

Surprisingly, both mother and child survived infancy and eventually I became quite confident on how to care for a tiny baby. But by the time that certainty came, my little one had become a toddler. That unique stage of mothering required a whole new set of skills and patience. I had only a very short span to conquer that phase and by the time I accomplished it, the child was a preschooler. This game of "tag you're it" continues to this day. I have always felt my level of expertise as a mother has been about six months behind.

I want my daughter to know that if God gives her the privilege of being a mom, He will also help her do what it takes to complete that job. I wish there were a comprehensive list of dos and don'ts for parenting that would guarantee success for the child, but there isn't. The goal of most Christian mothers is to see her child come to adulthood as a godly, productive person. In 3 John 4 we read, "I have no greater joy than this, to hear of my children walking in truth." If this passage is applied to motherhood, it is without question an absolute reality.

The following suggestions reflect some wisdom that has proven helpful in our family. Perhaps these ideas will encourage you and your daughter to delve into the truths, joys, and experiences of motherhood.

Love Them Enough to Discipline

Regardless of the problems society may have with some forms of discipline, God has the first and last word on the subject. We are told in Hebrews 12 that if we fail to discipline our children we are, in essence, communicating that we don't love them. Instead of citing scientific and personal opinions, I unashamedly point to the Word of God as the correct standard for such discipline. The Scriptures are clear that boundaries are essential and spankings are sometimes necessary. Let me encourage you to glean from the wisdom found in Hebrews 12:5,6,10,11; Proverbs 3:12; 13:24; 19:18; 22:6,15; 23:13,14.

Sit Together in Church

Some parents want their worship experience to be with "adults only." For this reason many churches have established a "children's church" program, segregating the congregation according to age groups. I understand the need to be able to concentrate on the service; however, when our children were very young I became convinced of the importance of them participating with us in "big church." The fruit of that decision to keep our children with us in church proved valuable beyond description, although inconvenient to me at times. In fact, I sat in the back pew ready, willing, and able to dart out the back door at the first indication that our children would be a disruption to those around us. As a result of sharing the worship experience together as a family our kids, when they were teenagers, actually opted to sit with us instead of with their friends!

Give Your Children Tools, Not Just Toys

Many tools cost more than toys, but they last longer and help foster a child's abilities and interest. For instance, musical instruments, art lessons, and even special mission trips to other countries are investments of monetary resources that help broaden a child's world.

Listen to Their Words, Read Their Expressions, Hear Their Hearts

Wise parents will be aware of the changing moods of their child. We must give our kids the freedom to express their fears and doubts. This is especially important as they get older and their problems have greater consequences. Topics such as sex and school and social concerns need our attention. One day Heidi called from college and tearfully asked, "Will you hate me if I flunk math?" I said, "No, I won't hate you. And by the way—you will not flunk math. Tell me what's wrong, honey." After she calmed down a bit, she explained the struggle she was having meeting the requirements of her math class. We discussed the problem and agreed on a possible solution. She decided she should drop out of the class for the time being, but she committed to taking the same math class during the summer session. With some extra effort on her part she came away with her pride intact and, later, a good math grade.

Create Healthy Relationships with Extended Family

Children can never have too many people in their corner, praying for them and holding them accountable for their actions. In keeping with this, Steve and I have made it a priority to make sure our kids are linked to our extended family, especially their grandparents. In order to preserve this attachment we have made it a point to always treat our parents with the utmost respect. Our children never heard their grandparents referenced in a disrespectful manner. We visited them, called them, and sent cards and gifts on appropriate occasions. It is very gratifying that even though our children are grown and away from home they still maintain contact with their grandparents. In this day of families living so far apart, it's even more important that we stay connected.

Allow Children to Be Part of the Family Work and Economy

In today's culture it seems like children are oftentimes regarded as a financial liability. It doesn't have to be that way. Everyone wants to feel like they contribute to the good of the family. Even though our music career meant Steve and I traveled frequently, we always included our children in our schedule. In fact, they were an important part of what we did. Nathan was recording by age three, and at ten he was helping to set up the sound equipment and run the prerecorded music tracks. When Heidi was five years old she began recording and singing in concerts with us. She also helped set up the book and music table. Both of them assisted with the "taking down" and packing up of the equipment after the evening service. Working together created a situation where we all felt like a team. Children not only need to be taught good work ethics, but they also need to feel important and productive.

Enjoy the Things Your Children Find Interesting

I've never figured out how our children ended up with such diverse musical tastes. As far as I'm concerned, if a selection doesn't feature at least one banjo and a mandolin it's not worthy of my listening.

When Heidi became enamored with Big Band music (Tony Bennett, Tommy Dorsey, The Andrews Sisters) I thought she'd fallen off the piano bench and hit her head. But her love of the 1940s music styles continued and intensified. Regardless of the twanglessness of her musical picks, I began to listen to it to share her enthusiasm. Before long I found myself not only wanting to like it, but enjoying it (to a degree).

Our son, on the other hand, loved loud, banging electric guitar music. So I had that spectrum of the music scales to climb as well. I can hear some of you laughing out loud (and loud is the operative word here) at my challenging musical adjustments. I know music can be a subject that divides and conquers many families. As a mother who has been there, I encourage you to not allow it to separate you and your child. As difficult as it may be, there are issues that can be ignored—and music is one of them.

Our parental guidelines concerning music were simple. If the music was not immoral or blasphemous then we would find a way to like it. We taught our kids to look at the complete picture. The lyrics of the songs were very important, but so were the lifestyles of the people performing the music. We encouraged our children to consider the following questions: Does the personal behavior of the performer honor God? Do the lyrics of the songs encourage us to live a godly life?

Prohibiting music without pointing out why it is unacceptable may actually provoke children to anger and open the door to rebellion. To be honest, I am much more concerned over some of the soft, sweet-sounding music that is popular today. Don't be lulled by the musical style. For instance, a lyrical song conveying the message that the love of self is the greatest form of love should be challenged. The song may be pretty, but the message is deadly.

Take Advantage of the Outdoors

Steve is an avid nature lover and, thankfully, he often included the children in his many adventures. My job as the "fraidy cat" mother was basically to keep quiet. Instead of giving in to my natural tendency to be fearful and apprehensive, I allowed Steve the freedom to develop his kind of father/child relationship. At times this involved Steve and the children spending the night in a small boat tied to an oil rig in the Gulf of Mexico, biking through the back country of Kentucky and Tennessee, and even hiking the Appalachian trail where grizzly bears like to eat curly headed daughters as afternoon snacks. Trusting in God and controlling my emotions was difficult but necessary if Steve was to have the freedom and joy of being an active dad.

Malachi 4:5,6 highlights the importance of a father's relationship with his children: "I am going to send you Elijah the prophet before the coming of the great and terrible day of the LORD. He will restore the hearts of the fathers to their children and the hearts of the children to their fathers, so that I will not come and smite the land with a curse." One of my major responsibilities as a mother was to support an active, strong relationship between Steve and our children.

Eat Dinner Together

A study done at the Cincinnati Children's Hospital Medical Center under psychologist Blake Bowden found that teens who eat dinner at home with their parents at least five times a week are less likely to be depressed, more motivated in their school work, and have a happier social life.[13]

I challenge you to create and maintain evening mealtimes. Make the adjustments in your family schedules so you can eat together. Remember, the family dinner table doesn't always have to be at home. Getting together and sharing a meal is the primary purpose. So if it's an impossible task to pull together a meal, go out for pizza or a burger—but be together and talk. Here are a few guidelines to help make family dinner times more effective.

Turn off the TV. According to one study, more than half of all Americans watch TV while eating dinner. With the television on, the benefits that result from eating together are wiped out. It's not the meat loaf and the mashed potatoes that have miraculous powers, it's *talking* and *reconnecting* with one another that is vital to our well being.

Let the phone ring. If you have an answering machine, let it do its job. If you don't have one, get one. There are very few calls that can't be returned 30 minutes later when your meal is over.

Get the family talking. Plan ahead by creating some upbeat and engaging conversation starters. The dinner table is not the place to bring up problems with bad grades, leaky faucets, or in-law conflicts. If the talk is unpleasant and hurtful, no one will want to be there. If you can make being together as a family an enjoyable experience, it will become something everyone looks forward to.

Have everyone present. Requiring every family member to be present may mean that mom and dad will have to make some choices and set priorities. Build relationships so that family members feel an obligation to show up because "it's just not the same when one member is missing."

Let Them Know You Pray for Them

Since our children were conceived, Steve has set aside Wednesdays as a day of prayer and fasting for them. In recent years I have joined him in that commitment. Our kids have always been aware that Wednesdays were different. In fact, the children seemed burdened as they realized their father was sacrificing food and comfort on their behalf. When the evening mealtime came and the fast was over, the heaviness lifted and there was a feeling of celebration. I made sure the children were aware of their father's commitment to prayer. I wanted them to know they were loved, but I also wanted them to realize the responsibility they had to be sensitive to the Lord. I sincerely believe Heidi and Nathan are walking with the Lord as a result of the prayers made on their behalf. It is also extremely gratifying to see our children setting aside Wednesdays as a day to pray and fast for their families. This legacy of prayer is a cord that binds us together, even during difficult times.

Motherhood Is Giving Them Wings

Letting go of our children is not an easy job. Do you remember what it was like when you were in the hospital preparing to give birth to your child? I don't know about you, but there came a time when it really hurt. I was doing the nonmedicated, Lamaze system of childbirth. That basically means you learn to breath heavily, leaving you so light-headed that you don't know your body is being ripped to shreds as you pass something out of your body the size of a bowling ball. Steve says Lamaze really works because he never felt a thing.

I remember as the head began to crown and the pain continued to increase thinking, "I change my mind. I don't want to do this. It hurts!" If I had fought the process, the baby would have died and eventually I probably would have, too. But because I was willing to endure the pain and allow the child to leave my body, becoming a separate person from me, the child came forth as a beautiful, independent individual who demonstrated the glory and creativity of God.

Years later, when once again it is necessary to let a child go there is a pain that is just as intense. However, if we refuse to allow him or her the freedom to live as an individual we run the risk of taking away our child's opportunity to allow the Lord to do His work in making him or her the unique person He created. Furthermore, an unwillingness to release our offspring has the potential to do great harm to our relationships. Steve wrote the following lyric years ago as he anticipated the struggle to set our children free.

The Arrow and the Bow

Here is wisdom for the moms and dads
That time has proven true
The day your children learn to walk, they start
To walk away from you

For at first you hold all of them
Cradled safely in your arms
Then one day it's just their hand you hold
And soon it's just their hearts.

And there'll even come the time
If your love for them is true
You'll have to let their hearts go free
To let them love someone else, not only you

Can the sparrow ever learn to fly
If the nest is all he knows
Can the arrow ever reach its mark by remaining in the bow
No, you have to let it go[14]

Though this song was written when our children were small, its truth has come to pass. My mother also understood the need to let go of me although it was extremely painful for her to do so. When I was accepted into Moody Bible Institute in Chicago, Illinois, I was only 17. I had never spent much time off the dairy farm in rural West Virginia, and I had no concept of how my life was about to change as I moved to the large city. At the time I was oblivious to anything except the excitement of the opportunity. Any danger or necessary adjustments were not part of my thinking.

It wasn't until I noticed that my mom hadn't gotten out of bed for three days that I started to see she was having a difficult time with my leaving. I didn't have enough sense to be scared but Mom did. Later she confessed how sick she was at the thought of my going away. I knew she was suffering, and yet not one time did she ever say a word to discourage me from going. Just as she put her own feelings aside and thought about my need for pursuing God's will, I want to do the same for my own daughter.

When a child is liberated from the confines of the home in which she was raised and has traveled a few years down the road of time, it is then she often looks back and clearly sees her mother's contribution to her life. Every mom looks forward to being the subject of the well-known Proverbs 31:28 NKJV compliment: "Her children rise up and call her blessed."

If allowing our daughters to leave for no other reason than to hear them say these words, perhaps it is worth it. My mother-in-law received her son's verbal reward in the form of the words that follow. They were written by Steve in his forty-third year.

A Mother's Touch

She could open up the pantry with hardly nothing there
And like the loaves and fishes there'd be plenty left to share.
She could take a penny and stretch it to a dime.
She could kiss a fever and leave us feeling fine.

There is only one explanation
for these amazing transformations
How she could take so little and turn it into much.
'Cause God gave her a miracle when He gave her
A mother's touch.

Give her two yards of cotton and a little bit of lace
She'd turn a "flower on the wall" to the prettiest girl in the place.
She could take a young man's heart that was drowning in his tears
And bring back the sunshine with just a listening ear.

And of all a mother's hands can do
Nothing can compare
To the way she could reach heaven
And touch a child's heart with her prayers.

There is only one explanation
for these amazing transformations
How she could take so little and turn it into much.
'Cause God gave her a miracle when He gave her
A mother's touch.[15]

6

Chicken 101

I want my daughter to know
God holds in high regard
the work she does as a homemaker.
He sees each act of service,
whether great or small,
as an essential part of creating
an atmosphere of love and
protection in the home.

To Be a Worker at Home

The day had finally arrived. Many preparations had been made and everyone was ready to go see the long-awaited, sweet grandbaby. The grandparents, along with the great-grandmother, wrapped and packed the presents and soon were on their way. The eight-hour drive seemed an eternity as they anticipated their arrival. They had patiently waited three weeks for the young mom to get adjusted to the hectic schedule of motherhood. Their son and daughter-in-law had bought their first home just three months before the baby was born, so everyone understood that the young woman needed the extra time to get her home organized and the baby established on a routine.

When the grandparents walked in they were taken aback by the appearance of the house. Boxes stood stacked against the wall of the living room just as they had during their last visit some weeks before. As they reached for the tiny baby they were met with the ammonialike smell of old urine. Even though it was closer to noon than morning, it seemed that the newborn was yet to have his bath and diaper change.

The grandmothers were more than happy to help bathe and dress their new grandson. The afternoon passed with lots of caresses, kisses, and conversations. Eventually it came time for dinner. The young father seemed at a loss when his wife indicated she hadn't prepared anything for dinner. The in-laws suggested they all go out or order food in. The more they insisted, the more evident their son's embarrassment became. He went to the freezer, pulled out a frozen casserole that some church ladies had brought over the first week the baby was home, and put it into the oven to bake. That evening's dinner consisted of the casserole and water.

Anyone who has ever experienced the overwhelming job of being a new mom can sympathize with this situation! As I listened to the grandmother tell the story, I felt more than compassion for the young mom. I was grieved for her. Someone had failed this woman. She obviously had not been trained in the area of being an efficient homemaker. She had a lot of new responsibilities; nonetheless, the humiliation she and her husband felt could have been avoided had some older woman, preferably her mother, taken the time to teach her how to prepare for company.

After speaking with the grandmother and hearing the frustration she felt from seeing her grandson living in such an untidy, disorganized home, I began to worry about the job I had done in preparing Heidi for her marriage.

For years I nagged and begged my daughter about her house-keeping—or should I say lack of such. As a teenager, Heidi was totally content to sit on her bed in utter filth and squalor, among clothes from the previous week's wearing piled nearly to the ceiling (do I exaggerate?). Was she preparing herself mentally for some mission trip to an impoverished third world country? No. She simply didn't see the need in making her bed *("It will be messed up in a few hours when I to go to bed, why make it?")* and hanging her clothes up *("I know where they are!")*.

My constant harassing and convincing arguments fell on deaf ears. If she saw no practical use for her domestic efforts, she didn't do them. A well-meaning schoolteacher once told her she should learn geometry so she would know how to install her very own in-ground pool. She replied, "If that's why I'm studying this subject, then I'll hire that job done." Thus, geometry went down the drain.

To be honest, I was concerned about Heidi's lack of enthusiasm for housekeeping. I feared this scant interest in a clean house would make her subject to surprise visits from the health department after complaints from her neighbors. My anxiety couldn't have been more unfounded.

I couldn't help but think about the grandmother and her grandson as I prepared to visit Heidi's apartment for the first

time. The evening was cold and rather snowy, but we had
promised to go to dinner at Heidi and Emmitt's. From the
moment we entered the front door any concerns as to whether
Heidi was capable of "keeping her house" were quietly put to
bed (which, by the way, was neatly made).

A clean house, a warm fire, and a delicious meal awaited us
as we entered the beautifully decorated apartment. Candles and
flowers adorned the nicely arranged furniture and a sense of
contentment filled our hearts.

Had my relentless badgering finally accomplished the desired
results of our first evening in Heidi's new home? Not really. I am
now convinced that my relentless nagging did absolutely no
good. Heidi *already* had the skills she needed to take care of a
home; all that was missing was the *reason* to do it. What was the
impetus she discovered? It was her house she was cleaning. She
wasn't doing what she was told to do by an overbearing mother,
she was preparing *her* nest. Heidi wanted her house to reflect
the way she felt about her newly established family.

Is housekeeping necessary or is it just the ravings of obsessive, antiquated mothers? The well-known chapter for young
women found in Titus 2 is quite clear that maintaining a clean,
orderly home is not only a good idea, but also a mandate from
God. Scripture instructs younger women to accept the training
offered by the older ones to "be workers at home." In an effort
to find some super-spiritual meaning to this well-known phrase,
I did a word study from the original Greek. I finally concluded
that the Titus 2:5 verse implies exactly what it says: "To be a
worker at home" means "to look after domestic affairs with pru-
dence and care." Does this mean God thinks the way we clean
and organize our homes is important? Absolutely. The work we
do at home is a *spiritual* responsibility. Colossians 3:17, 23 says:
"Whatever you do in word or deed, do all in the name of the
Lord Jesus, giving thanks through Him to God the Father....
Whatever you do, do your work heartily, as for the Lord rather

than for men." This passage was written for individuals who were put into service as slaves. But this admonition is even more true for those of us who have willingly taken on the responsibility of caring for family members we love and adore. The word "heartily" indicates we are to put our entire being into our housekeeping. There is no doubt that clean dishes may at times seem rather unimportant, but God rewards that menial task and accepts it as an act of worship to Him. Could keeping house be worthy of such a scriptural instruction? I think so.

Here are some housekeeping tips shared by some veteran homemakers. As you read these insights, keep in mind that as mothers we can give our daughters (and sons!) the expertise, but God gives them the motivation.

1. Carry your cleaning products and tools with you in a plastic carrier or an apron with pockets. This keeps your hands free for the cleaning jobs.

2. Use the same cleaning product for as many jobs as possible. This eliminates being bogged down with too many bottles and sprays.

3. Keep your cleaning tools and products in one place, refilling them as needed. Use them only for cleaning.

4. Work clockwise around your room, and go from the top to the bottom.

5. If something isn't dirty, don't clean it. Look at the mirror before you spray the cleaner on. If it's all right, go to the next task.

6. Space your furniture to make vacuuming easier. If you can't get the vacuum beside the bookcase, then move it until you can.

7. Change your cleaning cloths often. It doesn't do any good to clean if you are moving dirt from one place to another.

8. Be careful when you spray products on your furniture. Make sure they are safe for the surfaces before you use them.

9. Spray the cloth when you are cleaning small items. It saves time and spray.

10. Dust first, then vacuum—and do it often. Your best friend, when it comes to vacuuming, will be your long (25–50 feet) extension cord. The more dirt you keep off your floor, the less dirty the rest of the house will be.

11. Spend about 30 minutes each day doing the necessary things to give your home an orderly appearance. A house that is straight and uncluttered gives the impression that it is clean, even if it's not quite up to par.

12. If you only have time to clean one room, clean the bathroom that unexpected company might use. If your kitchen and bathroom can be maintained, it's easier to keep up with the rest of the house.

13. Do the job you hate to do first. Get it over with. Do not procrastinate. Stand at the door of a room and look around. Go from left or right and start picking up and putting things back in order until you come back to the door. Although some people feel an orderly home is unimportant, I have found that it sets the mood for all activities. We either create an atmosphere of peace or chaos.

14. Get rid of clutter. If you don't use it, then lose it! Garage sales are a redistribution center for clutter. One woman's junk is another woman's junk. Seriously, sell it or give it away, but get it out of your house if you don't use it. Of course, very often the rule of the game is "as soon as you sell it, you will need it," but that's what Wal-Mart is for.

15. Take advantage of helpful books on housekeeping. The library is full of great books by Emilie Barnes, and there

are magazine articles and columns such as "Hints from Heloise" that can be found in newspapers. One of the most helpful resources I've found is the book *Totally Organized* by Bonnie McDonough. I also have her *401 Ways to Get Your Kids to Work*. Great sources for ideas are friends. Ask if they have any helpful advice for keeping an orderly house.

16. Avoid the temptation to be lazy. When I was growing up I didn't invite friends over because I feared what the house would look like. I've tried to change this in my home. I want my husband to always be proud of how our house looks. The Bible has much to say about choosing industriousness over sluggishness. Much of the work God wants to accomplish in our houses must start in our hearts and minds. As we put Him as our priority and create a routine where He is given first place in our hearts, then He is able to work the needed changes in our daily routines.

17. Relax and enjoy life. Don't be consumed with a spotless house. There are more important things in life than this.

18. Overcome bad habits. Even if keeping your house is hard for you, reform your errant ways. If you make your bed as soon as you get up it can set the mood to do other things that need to get done.

19. Don't be quick to judge others. If your friend's house is out of order, there may be a good reason. If she seems open to your assistance, then lend a helping hand. Take her children for an afternoon, and let her work on getting her house in order. (If you go to a park or McDonald's playground you leave the mess behind when you take the kids home.) Remember, "People don't care how much you know until they know how much you care."

20. Don't nag your daughters (or sons) about their rooms. Give them the needed skills, but don't destroy your relationship

over whether the bed is made or not. Dust returns moments after you clean, but time with your children is gone forever. Choose your battles wisely and spend your time building your love relationship, not tearing it apart over a power struggle about who's going to win the war of the clean room.

Be Age Sensitive

Phyllis Diller said, "Cleaning your house while your children are still growing is like shoveling the walk before it stops snowing." As mothers, we should adjust our expectations to match the ages of our children. When my children were babies I desired to have one room that was not strewn with toys and equipment. I also feverishly worked to make sure my house never smelled of nasty diapers. Even though my home was never spotless, by setting daily goals I accomplished a lot. (It's important to guard against putting too much pressure on ourselves to fulfill unrealistic expectations. One mom said her goal at the end of each day was to have a clean house, the lawn mowed, the car washed, and her children sitting on the couch wearing white. If she ever does accomplish this she'll be a very tired woman!)

When our children are grown and gone, we have no excuse for having a messy house. Yet, I still find it difficult to keep things orderly, even though it's just Steve and me. Keeping house is not for the fainthearted. We need God's help to do the job correctly.

Giving Advice

Remember the story of the grandmother who was disappointed with the job her daughter-in-law was doing at keeping house? It raises a legitimate question: What should a mother do when she finds her daughter or daughter-in-law doesn't live up to even minimal expectations of what a good homemaker should be? My advice is simple: Keep your mouth shut. By the time your daughter is old enough to have her own house and family, your job is finished. If she doesn't have the skills she needs, she will have to find them elsewhere. If you have offered help and she chooses to not follow your instructions, then you both will have to live with the consequences. In like manner, if your son and his wife choose to not keep an orderly home, let someone else teach them. There are far too many interpersonal dynamics involved for the mother-in-law to occupy the position as critic.

Moms, bite your tongues and earnestly pray that God will bring someone into the life of your daughter or daughter-in-law to help her. And, please, do not buy her cookbooks or videos on how to be a good housekeeper. That is not only rude, but it can also be very unkind. These "gifts" can rarely be given discreetly, and the receiver will have no doubt as to what is being implied by these offerings.

There is one exception to this advice. If the young wife *asks* for assistance or instructions, then give it....carefully and sparingly. Remember, most women do not want another woman critiquing or criticizing them in any way.

I received this sweet poem from Steve's fabulous aunt, Nina Elkins. Perhaps it will inspire you as it did me to keep our work in perspective.

Excuse This House

Some houses try to hide the fact that children shelter there.
Ours boasts of it quite openly, the signs are everywhere.
For smears are on the windows, little smudges on the door;
I should apologize, I guess, for toys strewn on the floor.
But I sat down with the children
and we played and laughed and read;
And if the doorbell doesn't shine, their eyes will shine instead.
For when at times I'm forced to choose the one job or the other;
I want to be the homemaker, but first I'll be a mother.

These sweet words of an anonymous mother who had "chosen wisely" to care for her children and give her heart to her family reminded me of those times when I had foolishly chosen a clean house over spending time with my children. I remember instances when Heidi was growing up that I would avoid the very sight of her room. Sadly, even when her bed was made and her clothes were hung up (which happened more often than I gave her credit), she still didn't keep her room tidy enough for my high and sometimes unreasonable standards. It seemed but just a moment until the time came for her to leave home to go to college. The week before she left the two of us cleaned her room. We rearranged and organized things the way I wanted them. A few days after she was gone I noticed that I would go in and look around at how orderly and clean her room was. I soon realized no one disturbed the magazines that were neatly stacked on the shelf. Her bed pillows stayed fluffy; they were never squished and shoved off center. I finally had her room the way I wanted it. There was one problem. I wasn't at all happy. Heidi's room was indeed clean, but it was also empty.

There is a passage in Proverbs 14:4 that says: "Where no oxen are, the manger is clean, but much revenue comes by the strength of the ox." If today I had the choice between a "clean stall" (Heidi's bedroom) or the strength of the oxen (my sweet Heidi) there's no question which I would choose.

In a spirit of repentance for having been an overbearing, demanding mother who hurt her daughter's feelings on far too many occasions over this issue of a clean room, may I respectfully offer some advice to mothers who are in the midst of this seemingly endless battle?

1. *Realize "there's more than one way to do things."* Be sensitive to your child's feelings. Looking back I regret the many times I used a "know it all" attitude with my daughter.

When you find yourself instructing your daughter on how to do something, remember there is not *one* way to do it. Most methods are a matter of opinion or style.

2. *Admit "it's never too late to come clean."* Apologies are always appropriate. Like a lovely diamond bracelet, the color is always right and it always fits. If the need exists, apologize for the lack of a loving attitude. First Corinthians 13:5 TLB says, "Love does not demand its own way." The old adage "it's my way or the highway" is a result of unbridled, self-righteous pride. I leave this subject with one question for you: What is more important, building a loving friendship with your daughter or daughter-in-law or being right? The answer is obvious. Mercy should always win over judgment (see James 2:13).

7

Money Really Matters

I want my daughter to know how
to handle money. She needs to equip herself
with biblically sound financial knowledge,
cultivate a simple, childlike trust in God
as her provider, and fight the human
tendency toward greed.

He Who Dies with the Most Toys ...Is Still Dead!

When my children were elementary school age, I bought an excellent book at the local Christian bookstore. The title was *Kids Who Have Too Much* by Dr. Ralph E. Minear and William Proctor. I never found out which one of my children snatched the book and hid it from me, but I have my suspicions. However, as I began to scan the room for my reading material, I noticed the kids acting a bit strange. I'm not sure if moms are intuitively wise, plugged into the heart of God, or just looking for a fight, but I knew something was up. I confronted my little angels about the missing item. It didn't take long until they began to squeal on one another. What was the problem? They had hidden the book because they were afraid I might take away some of their stuff after I read it. It was only after I explained that the book also explored the quandary of children having too much stress and too much pressure on them that they were willing to hand it over.

How do we rightly supply the needs of our children from a maternal heart that wants to lavish material means on them without creating greedy, selfish, materialistic little "consumatrons"? The answer is not easy, and perhaps this is more of a challenge to those of us baby-boomers who have benefited from the hard work of our sacrificing parents. For the most part, post-World War II generations have had more opportunities for higher education, which lead to greater prosperity and financial security. Being the benefactor of a booming economy has left us with decisions and dilemmas our parents didn't face.

When I was growing up we always had the basics. We were not affluent enough to expect more or ask for more than necessary. Today, things have changed. Most families have fewer numbers of kids and, as a result, the financial pie can be divided into larger slices. Many well-meaning parents have created the predicament of producing children who not only expect more and more, but they usually get it.

There's a certain amount of envy I have of the limited resources of generations past. It would almost be a relief to be able to honestly say to my kids, as my parents did when we were growing up, "I'm sorry, we don't have the money." My reply as a youngster, based on my childish understanding of finances, prompted me to reply, "If you don't have the money, just write a check." This simpleton mentality used to be funny, but it's too close to reality nowadays to be humorous.

The modern version of this just-write-a-check solution is even more deadly because all we have to do is "use our plastic." As a result, we live in the most prosperous of all nations with the highest degree of indebtedness in the history of many generations. Saving account balances are at an all-time low, while credit card debt is soaring. (I have heard of families who borrowed money on their credit cards so they could invest in the stock market and then were hit hard by the recent Dow Jones losses.) The greediness, love of money, and preoccupation with our "stuff" is a legacy I'm afraid we have passed down to our children, leaving them ill-equipped to handle the inevitable economic slow down. Did you know the average freshman in college is in credit card debt to the tune of approximately $2,500?

Being Financially Wise

I was in the airport watching the TV monitors as the stock market was first approaching then passing the 10,000 mark on the New York Stock Exchange. The numbers would fluctuate teasingly close to the never before achieved number. The figures would reach 9,999 then dip down then pop over 10,000, only to dip again.

As the moments passed, the numbers topped the 10,000s and tiptoed over into uncharted territory. The count consistently and continuously climbed as I listened to the news commentator say, "It is impossible for the stock market to ever crash again." Suddenly, I felt a shiver run down my spine. I whispered a question to the man on the television screen, "Have you ever heard of the *Titanic?*" Some 75 years before, this beautiful luxury liner was christened "unsinkable." As all of us know, that ship is now lying at the bottom of the cold Atlantic Ocean.

What should we teach our daughters about money? Looking at what God has to say about it, its use, misuse, and its place in our lives is an investment that will have lasting yields.

The most familiar biblical excerpt about cash is found in 1 Timothy 6:10. Often this verse is misquoted as folks flippantly say, "You know, the Bible says 'money is the root of all evil.'" That's not what it really says. The correct quote is: "For the love of money is a root of all sorts of evil." It is the *emotion* we attach to the pursuit of the dollar that gets us into trouble.

In order to truly discover what God has to say about money, it is best to back up a few verses:

> But godliness actually is a means of great gain when accompanied by contentment. For we have brought nothing into the world, so we cannot take anything out of it either. If we have food and covering, with these we shall be content. But those who want to get rich fall into temptation and a snare and many foolish and harmful desires which plunge men into ruin and destruction. For the love of money is a root of all sorts of evil, and some by longing for it have wandered away from the faith and pierced themselves with many a pang (verses 6-10).

There are some key concepts I want my daughter to note as it pertains to our relationship with money. First, our goal is to *achieve godliness*, and we can only do so if we are content. What gets in the way of contentment? First Timothy 6:9 warns us that those who "want to get rich" put themselves in a precarious position of "a fall." "Fall," as used here, indicates a continuous downward motion. We have all heard about folks who get snookered by a con artist who promises huge returns for moderate investments. What makes people vulnerable to this trickery? Their *wants*. By desiring to become rich without working and managing their money, some people make themselves susceptible to these crimes. They want the security of wealth, as quickly as possible.

The Scriptures also point out that those who set their wanting on riches will *plunge* themselves into ruin and destruction. The word "plunge" means to be dragged, as in being pulled along the bottom of a pond. By setting their hearts on wanting money, they risk their bodies and souls.

Also, when we are focused on wanting material possessions we take our eyes off of what is really important. First Timothy 6:11 informs us of what is worthy of our efforts: "But flee from these things [turn aside from the desire for money]...and pursue righteousness, godliness, faith, love, perseverance and gentleness." Why would these qualities be more important to pursue than legal tender? The answer is in verse 17: "Instruct those who are rich in this present world not to be conceited or to fix their hope on the uncertainty of riches, but on God, who richly supplies us with all things to enjoy."

I often wondered why it was so wrong to want to be rich. I have concluded it is so abhorrent because it is born from an ungrateful heart. When we center our attention on what we don't have (lack of contentment) instead of all that God has given us, we are saying in essence, "God has not done it right." Benjamin Franklin made this observation concerning wealth: "Money never made a man happy yet, nor will it. There is nothing in its nature to produce happiness. The more a man has, the more he wants. Instead of its filling a vacuum, it makes one. If it satisfies one want, it doubles and triples that want another way. 'Better is little with the fear of the Lord, than great treasure, and trouble therewith.'" Putting our hope and security in money is to give ourselves over to an undependable master.

Beware of Debt

When Steve and I were just starting out we had a distinct advantage over what our children faced. We couldn't get credit even if we wanted it. One of the saddest moments for me in our early years of marriage was the day when we went to the store to buy a washer and dryer. I had fainted in a Laundromat while washing the clothes when I was pregnant with Nathan. Someone found me passed out cold on the concrete floor and called an ambulance. I'll never forget hearing the doctor tell Steve, "She is never to be in a Laundromat by herself again. She is susceptible to fainting and the heat of the dryers can set her off. You must be with her at all times."

Up until then, Steve didn't think we needed our very own washer and dryer. However, after doing the wash a couple of times by himself, he was convinced it would be much better if we bought the appliances. Since we didn't have the money for them, we decided to do the "all-American thing" and put our purchase on credit. We were prepared to make monthly payments.

I was so excited the day we were to get the appliances. We had just returned from a singing trip and called the store to arrange for delivery. My heart was broken when the store credit manager said he had run a credit check and we had none. It wasn't that we had bad credit, credit just didn't exist. I was devastated, but as I look back I praise God that we were refused the option of debt. We eventually saved our money and paid cash for less expensive models. Meanwhile, Steve kept popping the quarters and dimes in at the local washateria.

Nowadays, freshmen in college are sent credit cards by the handful. Young adults who have no income—or even the prospects of earnings—can get credit cards with generous limits. Steve and I were kept out of trouble because the system refused us. Young people today have the opposite situation. They must learn to spurn the snares set by the banking industry. There's a bumper sticker that spoofs a popular saying: "He who dies with the most toys...is still dead." What young people may not realize is that the pursuit of those toys may be what kills them financially.

Just as there were fewer opportunities for economic trouble when Steve and I were first married, there was also less help in how to manage our funds (or lack of them). Today there are many practical guides available in bookstores and even helpful advice on some radio programs. A valuable "money control" resource we gave to our children was the book entitled *Financial Peace* by our good friend Dave Ramsey. He has devoted himself to warning individuals of the heinous pitfall of depending on credit cards and avoiding the tragedy that results from living on more income than they make. In the earlier years of his career, Dave fell into the same mistakes he so enthusiastically rails against now. Having suffered through the loss of millions of dollars and filing for bankruptcy by the time he was in his 20s, Dave knows how to get into trouble, how to work out of it, and, best of all, how to *stay* out of it. Veteran money management experts like him are essential additions to a young person's resources for knowing financial peace.

Debt-Free Living

Steve and I have managed to live debt free for the past 15 years. How do we do it? From the beginning we learned to "make do" and spend less than we make even when we had to sacrifice our own comfort. As an example, for seven years we lived in a house where our only form of heat was a small free-standing, wood-burning Franklin stove. We heated the basement and allowed the heat to rise to the upper floor. In the cold of winter we would gather around the little stove to eat our meals, and at times we would even sleep in front of the stove to keep warm at night. In the summer we used fans and slept with the windows open instead of running an air conditioner. Steve and I realized we might be considered a little strange by doing things differently than our friends, but we were content. (We didn't realize just how out-of-step we were until the day some visitors came from out of town. We offered them the use of our house because we were out traveling and singing and would be gone for a few days. It never occurred to us that in the heat of the summer they might be a bit uncomfortable without any air conditioning. We returned home to find a note left on our kitchen table. It read, "Technology has advanced beyond what you are experiencing. Your house is like an oven, and we are going to a hotel." We laughed at that comment.) We knew we were living way below the comfort level of the average American, but until we could save up the money it was going to take to put in a heating and cooling system, we were going to continue to rough it.

When people determine to live debt free, it makes them seem like oddballs in this country where instant gratification has been elevated to the status of a national religion. The decision to live below their means genders some interesting reactions. On one occasion we had some friends over for dinner whom we hadn't seen for years. They had not yet visited us in our modest little house that we were in the process of fixing up. As the evening progressed, the man made a comment that I will never forget. He said, "I thought you would have been more successful than you are." As I contemplated his comment I realized it came from a man who was always trying business schemes and adventures. Some of them turned out to his good, but more of them had not been so successful. He and his wife had lived in beautiful houses, but they had also been bankrupt on several occasions. After they left, I looked at our house, car, and furnishings and concluded that as simple and unimpressive as they were, they were all paid for. Not many of our friends could make the same claim.

Learning to live within your means might mean you look less successful, and it also may make others feel uncomfortable around you. However, the fruit of the sacrifices are worth the peace of mind and the sense of accomplishment. There were times after a Bible study or Sunday evening church service when our friends went out to eat. Steve and I would leave the group and go home to cook dinner. Could we have squeezed the budget to accommodate an evening out? Perhaps. But the discipline we exercised at those times paid off. It did so even though we faced social ridicule and probably missed out on a lot of fun. Nonetheless, while others ran to the deeper end of the debt pool, we crawled closer and closer to our goal of financial peace because we believe that the borrower is indeed slave to the lender.

Convinced that financial responsibility demands that we teach our children to set as their goal to live within the income they make, we're aware that there are unseen situations that may arise. At those times a credit card can make the difference between, for instance, getting the car fixed or not getting home. We have temporarily gone into debt in those types of instances, but we've never made it a way of life. And our immediate goal in those cases was to always pay the bill as soon as possible. There is an acceptable use for credit cards—times of emergencies. In order to determine if it is truly a crisis or not, our rule of thumb is: If you can eat it or wear it, it's not an emergency.

Giving to God Is Not Optional

I want to encourage my daughter to consider her spiritual obligation to give to God's work. Malachi 3:8-11 is a "must passage" for every pursuer of righteousness:

> Will a man rob God? Yet you are robbing Me! But you say, "How have we robbed You?" In tithes and offerings. You are cursed with a curse, for you are robbing Me, the whole nation of you! "Bring the whole tithe into the storehouse, so that there may be food in My house, and test Me now in

this," says the LORD of hosts, "if I will not open for you the windows of heaven and pour out for you a blessing until it overflows. Then I will rebuke the devourer for you, so that it will not destroy the fruits of the ground; nor will your vine in the field cast its grapes," says the LORD of hosts.

The two main messages of the Bible concerning money could be narrowed down to 1) how to give to the poor and 2) how not to be poor. In this Malachi passage we are told how to avoid being devoured by the enemy by giving to God. The best defense against greed is generosity, the best demonstration of gratitude is liberality. In 1 Corinthians 16:2 we are given the following guidelines as to the New Testament pattern of giving.

1. *We are to give on a regular basis.* On the first day of every week we are instructed to bring our offering to God. At the time of the writing of this passage, most laborers worked for a daily wage. They were instructed to collect and save their offerings to bring in weekly.

2. *Each person is responsible to give.* No one is exempted from giving. We are to be good stewards of what God has given us, whether we make a lot or a little.

3. *We are to bring our offering to the storehouse.* The word used for storehouse means "a treasury chest." We are to bring our offerings to the church where the leaders can responsibly distribute the goods to the ones who are in need. There is order and accountability in this system. God wants our first fruits (we are to give from the top, not after everyone else is taken care of) because He deserves our very best. Giving is not exclusive to the church, but it should be included.

4. *We are to give proportionately.* As God has prospered us, we are to give. That indicates a percentage. In the Old Testament the tithe expected was 10 percent. Even though we're no longer under the law, that's a good place to start.

However, I don't believe we must stop there. If the Old Testament law demands that amount, I think New Testament grace deserves even more. For that reason many Christians give their tithe and then contribute to offerings above and beyond that amount. There is no way we can out give God. No matter the sums of our offerings, they will never be enough to show God the gratitude we feel for all He has done. God doesn't own 10 percent; He owns it all.

One preacher likened a good giver to the kiss a groom and bride share at the wedding altar. There are at least two similarities. First, they always want to do it. Second, you can tell they've done it before. God loves a cheerful giver.

As we recognize all that God has done for us and give generously, we will experience utter joy.

8

Mercy for the Mean

I want my daughter to know
how to deal with difficult people.

Be Kind and Be Wise

Of all the sage wisdom I could share with my daughter concerning getting along with nasty people, this is what it would be: Get used to it. They will always be around.

One of our family's favorite movies is the *television* version of the film *What About Bob?* (We even named our dog Bob after the main character.). Bill Murray plays a difficult person. In the first few minutes of the movie, Bob's original psychiatrist pawns him off on an unsuspecting colleague, Dr. Leo Marvin. After the first doctor got off the phone he began to shout, "Free! Free! Free!"

Well, there is one thing for sure—that shrink won't be free for long if he continues to associate with human beings. As soon as we "unload" one difficult person in our lives, be assured that another one will appear. It behooves us to learn how to deal with these people.

I've known my share of "Bobs." Years ago I had a friend I'll call "Jenny," whose friendship was quite exhausting. We had become acquaintances when our children were just babies. Steve warned me that she seemed to be the type of person who could be dominating. I did notice that she called quite often, sometimes four or five times a day. But I was also aware that she was lonely and had some serious challenges in her life. I thought I could help her.

Jenny had always had a severe weight problem. At 5'3" and topping the scales around 300 pounds, her health was beginning to suffer and she was desperate to lose weight. Having a great empathy for that particular struggle, I offered to help her in the endeavor.

Steve was going to be out of town for a week, so she and I agreed to fast together and pray for her situation. I had already lost the weight I needed to lose after Nathan was born; however, I wanted to be a support to her so I committed to fast with her the entire week. We agreed that she needed a spiritual break-through to destroy the stronghold she had given to food in her life. For seven days, I ate nothing. I got so thin I couldn't lay on my side because my bones didn't have enough padding. No matter how difficult it got, I believed the effort I was making was worth it.

One day she came to see me. As she walked into the house she seemed agitated. She could be quite hyper, so at first I didn't think much about it. Then she blurted out, "I refuse to feel guilty. There is no condemnation for those who are in Christ Jesus." I wondered what she was talking about. Then she continued, "I refuse to feel guilty for eating that box of doughnuts on my way over here. I did it and I'm not ashamed. There is no condemna-tion." She then went on to admit that she had not fasted during the week. Even though she had given in to hunger and decided the sacrifice was too hard, she neglected to let me know!

I loved Jenny, but that day it became obvious that I wasn't helping her. Although it seemed I cared more about her problem than she did, the real truth was that her situation was much more complicated than just excess pounds.

I learned an important lesson from that experience.

It is an unhealthy situation for all involved when one person tries to fix another. The person doing the "fixing" feels frustrated and the one being "fixed" feels controlled.

Coping Skills Required

Most of the difficult people who have disrupted my life have been invited in by me. Thankfully, they rarely pose a permanent threat to my tranquility. I've also worked with individuals who were jealous and thought I wanted their jobs. Others have been supervisors who thought the only way they could appear important was to squish people on their way up. With most of those individuals there was no lasting harm done.

Friends, fellow workers, and bosses can be temporary sources of irritations. However, it is family members who can inflict the most hurtful and long-lasting pain—and family tends to be around for a lifetime.

What do we do when the troublesome ones in our lives are those with whom we spend our holidays, attend weddings and funerals, or, even more challenging, sleep beside? Regardless of who the wearisome people might be, here are some coping mechanisms I've gleaned from women who have dealt successfully with such people.

1. *Consider the true source of the conflict.* If people are unhappy and hateful with others, be assured they are tormented by the enemy of their souls. We should see their meanness not as a reflection of who we are, but of the one who seeks to destroy all things good—Satan. Ephesians 6:12 encourages us to remember: "For our struggle is not against flesh and blood, but against the rulers, against the powers, against the world forces of this darkness, against the spiritual forces of wickedness in the heavenly places." If this is the source of the harm, then our prayers should reflect that battle as we enlist God's help on their behalf.

2. *Keep a positive attitude* even when those around you are mean and hateful. Be sweet. Even rhubarb can be tolerable if enough sugar is added! And remember, you can *always* learn something good from everyone.

3. *The response to their attack is our responsibility.* "A soft answer turns away wrath" (says Proverbs 15:1 NKJV). We can influence conversations with the tone and volume of our voices. Studies have shown that in a verbal conflict one party will often match the volume of the other. That

means if someone raises his or her voice to you and your answer is at a lower decibel level, eventually the other person will approximate it. When we respond with the same loud and spiteful spirit they have, we become as guilty as they are for the continuation of the conflict.

4. *You may be the only Bible they will ever read.* Consider your response as an opportunity to represent Christ in their lives. If you don't show mercy and restraint, they will not understand God's boundless love and forgiveness. First Peter 3:15-17 reads: "...Give an account for the hope that is in you, yet with gentleness and reverence; and keep a good conscience so that in the thing in which you are slandered, those who revile your good behavior in Christ will be put to shame. For it is better, if God should will it so, that you suffer for doing what is right rather than for doing what is wrong."

5. *If your difficulty is in a work situation* and the person is disrupting the productive environment, as kindly and discreetly as possible talk to someone in charge. If your supervisor is unaware of what is going on, he or she needs to know. If the offensive person is the boss, then you must decide whether you want to continue to inflict this disrespectful behavior on yourself. If you have done all you can do to get along and the person continues to be destructive to your life, then you must leave. You always have the choice as to whether you will put up with bad behavior. There are times when we must simply decide what peace of mind costs. If it costs us our jobs, so be it. The Scriptures instruct: "So far as it depends on you, be at peace with all men" (Romans 12:18).

6. *Avoid people who refuse to be peaceable.* Keep loving them, even when they are unlovable; however, don't put yourself in the situation where you have to be around

them. You can pray for them and be polite when you are in their presence, but limit that time as much as possible. This can be difficult, especially in the area of family life. You must manage the situation as best as you can in order to maintain peace.

7. *Avoid the pitfall of arguing with difficult people.* Trying to convince them they are wrong and you are right only leads to more frustration. "The anger of man does not achieve the righteousness of God" (James 1:20).

8. *Don't blame yourself for the way they act.* People are like boxes of crayons. They come in hundreds of colors... some bright and some dull. We cannot change anyone else; we are only responsible for the needed changes in ourselves.

9. *Always choose humility.* In James 4:6 we read: "God is opposed to the proud, but gives grace [greater grace] to the humble." As we pray for those who use us, we have the promise of God in Matthew 5:9,10: "Blessed are the peacemakers, for they shall be called sons of God. Blessed are those who have been persecuted for the sake of righteousness, for theirs is the kingdom of heaven."

Difficult Mother/Daughter Relationships

My relationship with my mother added a very special and positive component to my life. I am who I am largely because of the sacrifices my mom (and dad) made for me while I was growing up. For that reason, I found it nearly impossible to relate to the pain my friend was experiencing when she told me how much she dreaded her mother's impending visit.

She began to describe just how critical her mom had always been toward her. She said, "I know what I'm going to hear when my mother comes to see me. She's going to point out the extra

30 pounds I've packed on since last Christmas." In near tears, she continued, "I can't bear to hear her comments about my loud, misbehaving boys. And wait till she sees the color I painted the living room. That's going to engender a reaction." Oh, how sad to think that the difficult person in my friend's life is her very own mother.

As I saw the hurt look on her face, my heart ached for her to know the comfort of unconditional, accepting love. As a mother who is quite capable of being opinionated at times, I made a decision right then and there. I want my daughter to always be glad to see me. I have committed in my heart to never be critical of her. The time for teaching and correcting has come and gone. She is now an adult, and I will treat her as such. My daughter will have enough people in her life who will give her pause; I am going to make sure I'm not one of them.

Steve wrote a song about a difficult mother/daughter relationship. I offer the lyrics of this song as a timely warning.

She Still Rules Me from the Grave

On holidays and other occasions
I find myself having conversations
Talking to the memory
Of all the things she said to me

Like what to wear, and what to serve
I have ideas, but not the nerve
To do things if it's not her way
She still rules me from the grave

Now if you will, don't get me wrong
I have loved her all along
But when I'm talking to her memory
I'm so afraid to disagree

I have her blood, she has my soul
I have thoughts, she still controls
Does she know I feel this way?
She still rules me from the grave

I can see there's a line where love
No longer leads, but it starts to shove
She left me like a wounded child
Who'd die to see her mother smile

Now she's gone and I remain
And if I ever break the chains
I wonder if she'd feel betrayed
She still rules me from the grave

And what about this child I hold
What will she think, when I am old
And when I die, will she say,
"She still rules me from the grave?"[16]

The Special Mother-in-Law/Daughter-in-Law Relationship

I have joined a special sorority of sisters by becoming a mother-in-law. With this privilege and position, I feel a keen responsibility to be helpful to my daughter-in-law. I want her to know that of all the difficult people she may encounter in her life experience, I will not be one of them.

After so many jokes about the controlling, opinionated mother-in-law and the lazy, disrespectful daughter-in-law, I wondered, "Is it possible for two women who love the same man to get along?" My answer to this question is a resounding *yes!*

There are the horror stories we've all heard about interfering, nosy mothers-in-law. A friend of mine told me about hers who lives the next house up. She purchased a set of high-powered binoculars in order to spy on her daughter-in-law through the window. Even though my friend laughs about the antics of her misguided in-law, she is also hurt by such distrust and spitefulness.

There's no doubt I have been blessed of the Lord. Not only did I enjoy the most wonderful of mothers, but without question I also have the best mother-in-law anyone could have. She is the model of a godly woman; her life is worthy of emulation. In the same regard, the Scriptures give us a touching picture of the kind of relationship that can exist between a mother-in-law and a daughter-in-law.

Naomi and Ruth

The events in the book of Ruth took place during the time of the Judges, when Israel was in a state of spiritual confusion. That chaos is described in the sixth verse of Judges 17: "Every man did what was right in his own eyes." It was during this disturbing time that Bethlehem was afflicted with a famine. Elimelech, the husband of Naomi, made a fateful decision on behalf of his family. He decided that they would all move to Moab (modern-day Jordan) in order to find food.

By choosing to live in Moab, Elimelech changed the future of his family in many ways. Living in a foreign land limited his sons' choices for wives. At some point, the two boys married Moabite women. Eventually the father died and, tragically, ten years later the sons also died, leaving no children.

As I reflect on the life of Naomi, I feel sympathy for a woman whose dreams had been shattered. Not only was she a widow in a pagan land, but a widow without the monetary support of a father-in-law, sons, or grandsons. In her culture she was regarded as the most pitiful of all women. She was also left to care for two grief-stricken widows. Eventually, Naomi made the brave choice to return to her hometown. After she made this choice, she gave her daughters-in-law the freedom to return to their families. Realizing she had nothing to offer these women, Naomi said, "Return, my daughters. Why should you go with me?" (Ruth 1:11).

My heart was warmed as I read these passages. Naomi never referred to these women by their legal titles; she always addressed them as "daughters."

I'm sure you're familiar with the rest of the story. Orpah went back to her people, but Ruth chose to stay with Naomi. I wonder if Ruth's decision to stay with her mother-in-law was based primarily on the fact that Naomi was old and a widow. Or was it love? We get a glimpse of Naomi's state of mind when she arrives in her hometown in verses 20, 21: "She said to them, 'Do not call me Naomi [pleasant], call me Mara [bitter], for the Almighty has dealt very bitterly with me. I went out full, but the LORD has brought me back empty.'"

Naomi wasn't fully correct in the evaluation of her condition. Without question, she had suffered tremendous losses, but she was far from empty. Her life was enriched by the presence of her daughter-in-law.

Had Naomi chosen to do so, she could have rejected Ruth. After all, Ruth was of a different ethnic group, a different religion, and perhaps even of a different social/economic group. Yet Naomi fully accepted her son's choice. She loved and cared for Ruth, affectionately calling her "daughter." After the son was dead, the legal obligation was over. It wasn't the law that kept them related, however, it was love.

Both Ruth and Naomi are fabulous examples of the kind of strong women who are in-laws and able to deal with the sorrows and difficulties that are a part of life. Listed below are some attributes of these admirable women.

Ruth	**Naomi**
loyal—knew Naomi had no one else	*submissive*—yoked with her husband
teachable—followed instructions	*wise*—looked toward the future
industrious—asked for work	*accepting*—loved beyond reason
beautiful—washed, anointed, and dressed, making herself lovely	*courageous*—returned to her home

The end result of Naomi's decision to return to Bethlehem was the marriage of Ruth to Boaz, Naomi's kinsmen-redeemer. Ruth has the distinct honor of being named as one of five women listed in the lineage of Christ (see Matthew 1:5).

God Will Help Us

Whether the challenging people we deal with are strangers, friends, coworkers, bosses, or family, I want my daughter to remember that as we open our hearts to God's Word, we will receive the help we need to deal effectively and peacefully with those who are difficult. First Peter 3:8,9 encourages: "To sum up, all of you be harmonious, sympathetic, brotherly, kindhearted, and humble in spirit; not returning evil for evil or insult for insult, but giving a blessing instead; for you were called for the very purpose that you might inherit a blessing."

If the suggestions and ideas that I've shared prove ineffective, I have one last thought. When it comes to winning over a difficult person, try baking them cookies. This may sound trite, but few people can resist homemade chocolate chip cookies. You will literally have them eating out of your hand. (It seems to work every time for me!)

9

Courageously Facing Fear

I want my daughter to know courage
is not optional. If she conquers the temptation
to give in to fear and worry, she can deal
effectively with all other renegade emotions.

Walking a Well-Worn Path

Have you heard this adage? "Do not pray for an easier life. Pray to be a stronger person. Do not pray for a task equal to your power. Pray for power equal to your task." This is the attitude we need to cultivate to deal effectively with emotions that tend to undo us.

When it comes to conquering the paralyzing effects of fear, a good source of inspiration is found in courageous women. I want my daughter to know there are women who have provided an example of what it takes to navigate the rough terrain and the scary crossroads of this journey called life.

Courageous Women in the Family

If my daughter needs courageous role models, she need not look any further than her own family tree. On the cover of one of our music projects, "This House Still Stands," is the picture of a special couple. The man, Charles Elias Halblieb, is my maternal great-grandfather along with his wife, Susan Emily Duncan Halblieb. We used their picture on the CD cover to illustrate that longevity and faithfulness are possible even in the face of adversity. In the photograph, this couple is standing in front of a four-room house. In that dwelling they raised 12 children.

When my great-grandfather was a boy living in Germany, his mother (my great-great-grandmother) put him on a boat and sent him to America. As I contemplate my great-grandfather, my mind turns to his mother. What kind of love did it take to send a 14-year-old boy away, knowing she would probably never lay eyes on him again? As the family story goes, in the Jewish community where my relatives originated, the authorities were taking young boys as soldiers against their wills to man the army. In order to protect him from the ravages of war, his mom sent him away.

139

She gave him up so he could be free. So, with no money, no family, and no understanding of English, he came to America and settled in a small community in West Virginia. As a result of her decision, my great-great-grandmother's courageous blood flows through Heidi's and my veins.

There have been many brave women on both sides of Heidi's family who have blazed a trail of courage. Her maternal great-aunt Zara Williamson (my father's sister), left an impoverished home at age 15. Lying about her age, she enlisted with the nursing corp. At age 18, she joined the army during World War II, risking her life to minister to wounded soldiers.

Heidi's paternal great-grandmother, Easter Daisy Chapman, proved her courage when she found her seven-year-old son on fire. He had backed up to an open grate and the flap of his pajamas ignited. Rolling him on the floor, she extinguished the flame, but not before it burned his body from his hips to his shoulders. With no burn units or hospital available, she kept the boy at home and tended to his wounds. For over a year, the lad lay on his stomach as his mother bandaged and stripped the charred, rotten flesh from his back. She tirelessly nursed him back to health, showing no sign of waning even though she was the mother to 11 other children.

Maude Godby Steele, Heidi's other paternal great-grand-mother, left a legacy of a different kind of courage as she quietly endured the pain of stomach cancer. For two years she suffered yet never offered a word of discouragement or anger. Her daughter, Heidi's grandmother Lillian Chapman, said, "My mother left an example for me to follow, but I'm not sure I'm up to the challenge. When neighbors came in to visit her when she was sick they would grab their backs complaining of every ache or pain. My mother would comfort them, never uttering a sound about her own suffering. She was in so much agony they eventually had to operate and cut the nerves to her stomach. Even with the surgery, her pain persisted...and so did her quiet acceptance."

Heidi watched as my mother bravely contended with the devastation of cancer for years. For more than a decade, mom endured chemotherapy that kept the disease at bay until the spring of 1996, when she finished her work, laid it all down, and went home to be with the Lord.

All those women whose blood flows in Heidi's veins would have been proud of her because she, too, shows the promise of great courage. As a teenager she demonstrated her heart and heritage by stepping up to sing at my mother's, and later at my father's, funeral. With a voice as clear as a bell, she stood in front of everyone and honored the Lord and her grandparents.

Courageous Women in the Bible

Our family hasn't cornered the market on brave women. Role models demonstrating courage are plentiful throughout the Bible. The real-life stories shared throughout the Old Testament are there for a purpose. First Corinthians 10:11 says: "Now these things happened to them as an example, and they were written for our instruction, upon whom the ends of the ages have come." Also Romans 15:4 shares: "For whatever was written in earlier times was written for our instruction, so that through perseverance and the encouragement of the Scriptures we might have hope."

Following the mandate to read and learn from the saints of old, let us look at four brave women.

Deborah, the Prophetess and Judge

When it comes to gutsy, stalwart women, Deborah has to be at the top of the list. Her impressive résumé rivals any of today's most influential people. Even Sandra Day O'Connor, who served as the first female United States Supreme Court justice, has not accomplished the extraordinary feats of Deborah.

What a list of duties and credentials Deborah claimed. Her first title was that of "wife to Lapidoth." A homemaker by trade, her wisdom and judgment brought her to prominence among her peers. She was also described as "a mother in Israel" (Judges 5:7) before she became a judge. Some scholars assume "the mother" title was symbolic of her concern and care for the children of Israel. That may very well be. I, however, lean toward her actually being a mommy to a child. Where else would she gain such wisdom and understanding of the rewards and consequences of life? There's a good reason older women are to be the teachers, for they draw from a life that has experienced God's faithfulness. Jewish women considered barrenness a shameful situation for a married woman. There was a social stigma attached to being childless as was demonstrated in the Scriptures. (See Sarah, Genesis 11:30; Rebekah, Genesis 25:21; Rachel, Genesis 29:31; Hannah, 1 Samuel 1:5; Elizabeth, Luke 1:25.) For that reason, I'm inclined to assume that she was actually a mom.

If being a wife, mother, and judge were not enough to keep her busy (wouldn't you like to see her daily schedule?) she was a leader at a time when no one wanted to be led. Judges 17:6 tells us "every man did what was right in his own eyes." Being a moral compass in a culture of aimlessness and anarchy was no easy job.

During Deborah's judgeship, King Jabin was harassing the Israelites. With a weakened military and a famine of leadership, Deborah rose to the occasion. Being the voice for God, she prophesied His plan. Obediently, she called Barak from the tribe of Naphtali and instructed him to raise up an army to battle the Canaanites. But Barak wimped out. Refusing to proceed unless Deborah accompanied him, she took on the job of recruiter as well as battle strategist.

There is a spot in my heart that is warmed at the very existence of such an accomplished woman. She deserves recognition as a courageous person who probably did not seek out prominence and position but was willing, when enlisted, to serve nobly.

What more could this lady do? After the battle was won, she wrote an award-winning song about it. You can find it in Judges 5. Move over "music row" in Nashville—Deborah's in town!

Abigail, Protector of the Household

The first thing we learn about lovely Abigail is that she is a woman of intellect and beauty (see 1 Samuel 25:3). Second, we find she is married to a miserly man named Nabal. He was a descendent of Caleb, but he didn't carry any of the nobleness of his forefather. Abigail's husband is described as a wealthy, worthless, disrespectful, self-centered, greedy man. First Samuel 25:25 says it well: "He is a fool—just like his name means."

Although many women today may choose to marry men such as Nabal, Abigail probably had no choice in the matter. Marriage at that time and in that culture was a decision made by the father of the bride without her consent and often for monetary reasons. Witnessing her heart of discernment and dedication, I can't imagine she would have ever been attracted to such a harsh man as Nabal.

The story goes that some men came to Nabal and respectfully requested necessary food for David and his soldiers. The response the men received was, "Who is David? And who is the Son of Jesse?"

Nabal knew perfectly well who David was. David's men had protected Nabal's herds and fields some time earlier. Here he is deliberately insulting David.

A servant of Nabal found Abigail and explained the insult inflicted by her husband. Abigail also learned that David was riding toward her home with the express purpose of wiping out the household.

The following "D's" chronicle the courageous acts of Abigail, which ultimately God used to alter the course of her life.

Discerning. Abigail assessed the situation as volatile. She determined what it would take to defuse it.

Decisive. She planned specific steps of action. Realizing what she needed to do, she gathered up and prepared food then arranged for it to be transported to David's men. She didn't wait for David to come to her.

Deliberate. Abigail assessed, prepared, then acted. She *hurried* to David, fell at his feet, and made her appeal for mercy and forgiveness.

Diplomacy. Though unfounded, she took the blame for what her husband had done. David was angry at Nabal, but seeing this beautiful, intelligent woman humbling herself and shouldering the responsibility for the insult, David's anger was defused.

Delivered. The result of acting immediately and courageously resulted in the safety of her entire household. When she arrived home from this exhausting episode she found her worthless husband throwing a party. There was no food for the future king in the heart of Nabal, but plenty for himself.

Death. Abigail did not try to hide what she had done. She did, however, wait until the next day when her husband was sober to give him an account of her intervention. Scripture tells us at that point he died.

David. When David heard about what happened and that Abigail was a widow, he sent for her and took her as one of his wives. David rejoiced that he didn't seek revenge on Nabal, but that God had avenged his insult.

Esther, Deliverer of a Nation

During the news report frenzy surrounding the horrible murder of the precious little six-year-old girl JonBenet Ramsey, the public awareness of beauty pageants, especially for children, was piqued. There are a lot of mixed feelings about the wisdom of such beauty contests. Some people who feel favorably toward them point out the advantages many young women experience as they build self-esteem, receive scholarships, and enjoy monetary prizes. Others criticize and find demeaning the emphasis that is put on judging a woman according to her outward appearance.

Regardless of which side of the issue you come down on, Queen Esther won the biggest of all beauty contests. Without question, she was quite lovely—the most appealing of all the maidens. It is also obvious to all who read this account that she was much more than a pretty face and a shapely form. She was a woman of incredible wisdom and courage. Faced with the choice of risking her own position and safety or saving the Jewish people from annihilation—she stepped out boldly.

There are two well-known passages that capture the essence of this woman. Esther 4:14 says, "And who knows whether you have not attained royalty for such a time as this?" And 4:16, "And thus I will go in to the king, which is not according to the law; and if I perish, I perish." It is this kind of fortitude I hope my daughter will imitate.

Rizpah, Protecting Her Children

A recurring theme rings true throughout the Old Testament: Most women had absolutely no control over their lives. Being given in marriage to men they had never met and didn't love was commonplace. Their job was to give comfort, sex, children, and service to their husbands.

No helpless figure is more noteworthy than the sorrowful Rizpah. A concubine to King Saul, she bore him two sons, Armoni and Mephibosheth. Although she was afforded some protection by Mosaic law, she was easily discarded because of her status.

After the death of Saul and the crowning of David as king, we read of this lady. At the time, a dreadful famine gripped the land of Israel. David searched for the reason God was dealing harshly with His people. After conferring with the Gibeonites he learned of Saul's violation of an ancient covenant. To avenge this wrong the Gibeonites required the death of seven of Saul's descendants.

Among the seven hanged were Rizpah's two beloved sons. As if the killings were not enough, the bodies of the slain were left hanging, which added insult to the injustice. It was a shameful violation of God's mandate that "if a man has committed a sin worthy of death and he is put to death, and you hang him on a tree, his corpse shall not hang all night on the tree, but you shall surely bury him on the same day (for he who is hanged is accursed of God)" (Deuteronomy 21:22,23).

The blatant disrespect shown to her two dead sons was unbearable. Rizpah refused to leave their bodies hanging in disgrace and unattended. This loving mother was helpless to stop the killings, but being a courageous woman, she was determined to honor them afterward.

The executions took place around Passover, which would have been in March or April. Rizpah kept her vigil until the fall rains came in October or November. For up to six months she sought to protect her sons' bodies. Second Samuel 21:10 tells us: "And Rizpah the daughter of Aiah took sackcloth [a sign of mourning] and spread it for herself on the rock, from the beginning of harvest until it rained on them from the sky; and she allowed neither the birds of the sky to rest on them by day nor the beasts of the field by night."

When word reached King David of the relentless dedication of this grief-stricken mother, he was moved with compassion. He removed the bodies and gave them an honorable burial. (Likewise, he had the bones of King Saul and Jonathan brought back to the land of Saul's father. There, the former king and his son were buried together in the tomb of Kish.)

In an indirect way, Rizpah's courage was also noticed by Jehovah. Because of the diligence of this woman, King David was motivated to honor the remains of Saul and his sons. Thus, "God was moved by entreaty for the land." One woman's love for her children changed the heart of the king of Israel and, consequently, touched the heart of the King of kings.

Courageous Women of Today

Courageous women are not only found in the archives of our family history or the pages of the Bible. I know some modern-day women who have lived through extraordinary circumstances, facing them with the courage of a lion and the determination of a badger. These are the kind of women I want my daughter to know.

A Mother Finds a Way

Margaret Bubik, from Mesa, Arizona, is truly a courageous woman. She has inspired me with her dedication to her family and the tenacity with which she helped her daughter Tiffani. (Margaret would be the first to admit her success was a joint one with the family and friends who helped.) The bravery she has shown and her willingness to put the needs of others beyond her own warrants acknowledgment.

As a result of having gestational diabetes during her second pregnancy, Margaret was subjected to several interventions and medical procedures. As a result of the complications of one of them, Tiffani, born four weeks premature by Cesarean delivery, suffered a loss of oxygen, which resulted in a brain injury.

Margaret thought things were not quite right from the beginning. She found it disconcerting that Tiffani didn't cry upon birth.

Then she noticed she wouldn't nurse and her eyes seemed to wander, never focusing on a specific object. Each time it was brought to the attention of the pediatrician, she was told, "This is to be expected with premature babies. Don't worry, she'll grow out of it."

She didn't grow out of it; she got worse. Tiffani never creeped on her belly or crawled on her hands and knees. Along with underdeveloped motor skills, she also acted in a socially awkward manner and often made inappropriate noises.

Eventually the doctors acknowledged the problems. Tiffani had a severe learning disability, developed Tourette's Syndrome, and was diagnosed with Attention Deficit Hyperactivity Disorder. The child was put on many medications including Ritalin and Dexadrine. Other health complications included being mildly autistic, suffering hearing loss, and failing to acquire basic verbal skills. In fact, her vocabulary consisted of only five words by the time she was three years old.

Margaret became a woman with a cause. She was determined to find solutions for Tiffani's difficulties even though the medical community offered her no hope of improvement for her daughter's life.

Things began to dramatically change in one area when Margaret realized some of Tiffani's problems were due to a severe milk product allergy. With an adjusted diet, Tiffani's hearing problems diminished and her vocabulary improved. She was put on a very strict food program, which included avoiding all artificial colors, preservatives, artificial flavors, and all dairy products. Margaret was a persistent, loving, courageous mother. One day, while watching the TV show "Miracle Babies," Margaret and her husband, Bobby, saw a possible way to help their daughter. They began to investigate this option.

Although it took a long time to track down the facility mentioned on the show, they finally made contact with The Institute for the Achievement of Human Potential located in Philadelphia,

Pennsylvania. This organization offered them their first glimpse of hope that Tiffani could lead a productive life. Margaret and her family dedicated their efforts to following the rigorous recommendations from the professionals at the institute. Margaret writes,

> This program is an answer to prayer! Finally, after eleven years of searching and running into "brick walls," Tiffani is on the road to her miracle—being healed! Because this program is so very intense, I have resigned my position as ministry director at our church. It takes 10 to 12 hours every day, seven days a week, to do all that is required for her. Whenever I begin to feel overwhelmed, God shows me one more thing (no matter how big or small) that Tiffani can do that she has never been able to do before, and I realize that He will give the strength to do what is needed. He is so faithful.

The sacrifices Margaret and her family made have paid off. Margaret's day starts at 6:30 in the morning and finishes at 8:30 at night without any days off, but progress is noticeable! The many months of neurological "patterning" (learning to crawl and establishing new patterns in her brain to help her brain reorganize and perform its normal function, reflex masking, inhalations, intelligence programs, gnostic sensation development, a nutrition program, and more have offered glorious results. Tiffani is catching up with her peers in her schoolwork and has recently authored and illustrated her first book: *Moths and Butterflies!* God is so good!

Tiffani says, "When I grow up I want to help other brain-injured children." It's exciting to see a girl following in her mom's courageous footsteps.

The Naked Truth About Fear

Another courageous woman is one of my dearest friends, Kim Bolton. Kim and her husband, Tony, sing and conduct worship concerts that glorify Christ and edify the church. She is also a gifted communicator who speaks at women's conferences all across America. She has graciously given me permission to share this story.

Kim and Tony have been doubly blessed. They have two lovely, nearly grown daughters. In Kim's early 30s her body began to show signs of early menopause. The doctor confirmed Kim's suspicion. She began to make adjustments both mentally and physically for the "change" that was obviously taking place. One dramatic event she failed to anticipate came along nine months later. His name is Marshall. Then, within a couple of years, Reese made his arrival. The doctor was right about one thing: Kim's life had changed! She went from having independent daughters to being a mother to two boys who have been the delight of the whole family.

During those early years of parenting, Kim and Tony developed a system. They each shared the nighttime interruptions by dividing the night into shifts. Kim's shift was from ten o'clock at night until three in the morning. Tony would take the early morning hours from three to seven. This way both were assured at least a few hours of uninterrupted slumber.

One night Kim was awakened by a crying baby. She dutifully got out of bed and proceeded to rock, sing, and cuddle the bundle for some 90 minutes. Finally, at 3:30 the baby drifted back to sleep. Kim staggered to her bed and was in a cozy state of near repose when she heard the sound of feet coming down the hall. Too exhausted to even turn over and assuming it was her child, she simply moaned, "Get in bed with me." There was no response. She said it again, "Come on, crawl in the bed."

Again there was no movement. Curious as to which one was standing in her room, she turned over to see who it was. To her shock and astonishment she saw the rear end of a man laying on the carpet beside her bed. Not believing her eyes, she looked again. With his head and knees on the floor, this stranger's white hiney was perched up into the air.

Kim, stunned and startled, attempted to rouse Tony from his sound sleep. Assuming she was waking him up for his morning shift with the baby, he ignored her efforts. Finally she punched him hard. He turned over to see what the problem was and laid eyes on what Kim had seen moments earlier. They asked each other, "Who is this naked man in our bedroom?" As they queried in unbelief, obviously the disrobed intruder could hear them. Tony jumped out of bed with the intent of a major confrontation.

As Tony approached him, the prowler flung the phone, hitting him in the face. Tony, dazed and bleeding, faltered long enough for the man to dart out the front door.

Unsure that he was working alone, the Boltons began to look under the beds and in the closets. They soon discovered that the trespasser had ripped out all of the phone lines and had vandalized several rooms in their house. Assured they were safe for the moment, Tony went next door and called the police while Kim began to assess the damage.

With the kitchen so ramshackled, the family wondered how he could have done so much damage without garnering attention. Had Kim heard him during her 90-minute vigil? She heard the noises but she did what we all do—assigned duties to the sounds. "Oh, that's the ice maker," or "the air conditioner just kicked on."

Kim found it impossible to recover from the intrusion. She felt violated, unsafe, and angry at everyone in general—but Tony in particular. She began to accuse him, "Why can't you protect us? How could you have let him get away?" Her world began to unravel. She couldn't sleep at night. She walked the floor "keeping watch over her flock by night" (sorry, wrong story). Two weeks later, while doing laundry at two o'clock in the morning, she heard a sound at the front door. The intruder was back trying to break in again.

This time Tony was ready. When he opened the door, the man ran away. Every fear in Kim began to escalate. He had come back. Her paranoia increased as did her anger. Fear took over any rational thought. By now she was convinced no one could protect her and her children.

Each passing day, things got worse. By the sixth week of nursing a bitter attitude toward Tony and displaying obsessive behavior, her husband said, "Kim, you've got to do something about this fear and anger. It grows every day. Fix it, 'cause I've had it."

Decision day had come. Kim had to make a choice. She could continue to allow fear and anxiety to dominate her life and destroy those around her or she could practice what she believed. Desperate for help, she went to the back of her Bible to the concordance. She earnestly studied every Scripture on fear, peace, and sleep. She didn't just read the passages, she wrote them down. Then she started carrying them around in her pocket during the daytime. At night she literally pinned the Word of God to her nightgown. As she covered herself with the truth, the lies began to fall away. When the suffocating fear would come upon her and the voices of doubt and violation screamed in her ears, she began to talk back! But this time instead of her words reeking with hurt and doubt there was power in what she said. When she felt like a frightened child and all alone, she reassured herself with words from Isaiah 43:1,2:

> But now, thus says the LORD, your Creator, O Jacob, and He who formed you, O Israel, "Do not fear, for I have redeemed you; I have called you by name; you are Mine! When you pass through the waters, I will be with you; and through the rivers, they will not overflow you. When you walk through the fire, you will not be scorched, nor will the flame burn you."

At night, when she'd hear a sound that started her heart racing, she would cling to the fact of Psalm 91:11: "For He will give His angels charge concerning you, to guard you in all your ways."

Instead of listening to the accusations from the enemy that her husband was helpless, the police were incompetent, and the locks weren't strong enough to keep danger away, she put her confidence in the truth of Psalm 56:3: "When I am afraid, I will put my trust in You. In God, whose word I praise, in God I have put my trust; I shall not be afraid. What can mere man do to me?" Kim was sure that Hebrews 13:5,6 was and is true: "He Himself has said, 'I will never desert you, nor will I ever forsake you.' So that we confidently say, 'The Lord is my Helper, I will not be afraid. What will man do to me?'"

As she began to live in the truth of the Word of God, slowly but surely she could sense the change begin to happen. Her circumstances hadn't altered. In fact, three months after the first invasion the man came back. That time he was spotted before he could get near the house.

"When the Word of God does its divine work in your heart, your perspective changes," Kim declared. "All along I had been upset with the fact that the naked man got so close to me, I could have touched him. After God began to reveal the strength and power of His Word and His protective presence, I realized I could touch him, but *he couldn't touch me.*"

She began to recount all the ways God had protected her. Although the unclothed man had opportunity, he hadn't physically attacked her. He walked right past her children's room, and they were left unharmed. There was even $68 sitting on a table that was not taken.

The first time, he invaded the house. The second time, he couldn't get past the front door, and in his third attempt he wasn't able to get into the yard. God was there all along, taking care of His children and teaching them to trust.

Kim chose to put fear aside and embrace love. She chose her love for God over the anxiety that sought to destroy her. Fear and love cannot exist in the same person. First John 4:18 says: "There is no fear in love; but perfect love casts out fear, because fear involves punishment, and the one who fears is not perfected in love." The truth of Isaiah 30:18 took root, booting out the apprehensions and anxiety: "Therefore the Lord longs to be gracious to you, and therefore He waits on high to have compassion on you. For the Lord is a God of justice; how blessed are all those who long for Him."

True Courage

If my daughter can conquer the temptation to give in to fear, she will truly be courageous. How grateful I am that I can stand with my daughter today and look back through time at some incredible women who have faced and conquered difficult circumstances. I want Heidi to know that observing past victories will strengthen her in the future when she, too, will face tough times.

It was courage that moved David from the shepherd's field to the battlefield to fight Goliath. It was courage that moved Esther from the powder room to the king's throne room to plead for her people. And it was courage that moved Jesus from the garden to the cross to die for our sins.

I want my daughter to know that courage is not optional, and neither is it a personality trait. In essence, courage is not the absence of fear but proceeding in the face of it. Courage is essential if we want to walk with God and obey His voice.

10

A Shining Finish

I want my daughter to know that
living her life devoted to Christ
with a faithful heart is the greatest legacy
she can leave to those who come after her.

Encouragement for Life's Marathon

Susanna Wesley, mother of 19 children (including John and Charles) said, "Children, when I am gone, sing a song of praise to God."

In the ancient Greek games, marathon runners raced for the coveted wreath of victory. However, they didn't compete in the same manner as our modern-day athletes, where the first to cross the finish line is the winner. The racers of old would run carrying a lighted torch held high above their heads. The victorious contestant was the one who crossed the finish line with his torch still burning.

In these final pages I want my daughter to be encouraged as she participates in her life's marathon. In order for her to finish her race with her light shining brightly she must guard against these three things.

Don't Let the Past Defeat You

Pastor Jeff Wickwire, senior minister of the University Chapel in Fort Worth, Texas, says there's a reason the rearview mirror is smaller than the windshield. The rearview mirror was not designed to be used for forward movement, but merely to offer a reference point. We know if we drive looking backward, sooner or later we are bound to crash. The same is true as we maneuver down life's highway. If we keep our eyes firmly fixed on the past, whether concentrating on our successes or our failures, we will never reach the destination God has in mind for us. The apostle Paul wrote in Philippines 3:13,14: "I do not regard myself as having laid hold of it yet; but one thing I do: forgetting what lies behind and reaching forward to what lies ahead, I press on toward the goal for the prize of the upward call of God in Christ Jesus."

It is a powerful temptation to allow ourselves to be buried underneath the guilt and regrets of the past. We are wired in such a way that we are emotionally and spiritually affected by the things we have done. However, guilt is like a fever. It has a positive purpose. A fever tells us an infection is present in our bodies and medical attention is necessary. In the same way, guilt alerts us that there is a problem in our spirit that needs our attention. The godly sorrow we feel when we have done something wrong leads us to a repentance of heart and, consequently, a change of behavior. Once that is accomplished, guilt is no longer necessary. Holding on to the brow-beating and self-abasing emotion of guilt is destructive to our lives and can thwart the fulfillment of the will of God.

There are two women in the Old Testament who did not allow their past failures to determine their future. Let's briefly examine the choices made by Rahab and Bathsheba because they exemplify the wisdom of forgetting the past.

Rahab

There is no denying that Rahab had the worst of reputations. Three times the Scriptures refer to her as a harlot (a prostitute). I'm sure she suffered the moral and social repercussions of her trade.

We first read about Rahab when Joshua, the leader of the Israelites, sent spies into Jericho to scope out the situation and assess the possibility of a successful military campaign. The two men who were sent found themselves in Rahab's house seeking refuge. She had heard about how God had delivered the children of Israel out of the land of Egypt by literally drying up the Red Sea and given victory to the Israelites over the neighboring cities. Rahab declared to the two men, "When we heard it [the deliverance by the hand of God], our hearts melted and no courage remained in any man any longer because of you; for the LORD your God, He is God in heaven above and on earth beneath."

With that declaration of faith and putting her trust in God, she hid the spies and tricked her own people so the undercover agents could escape. Rahab showed her true heart when she courageously aligned herself with the people of God, making a deal with the spies that she and her family would be spared in exchange for her helping them defeat Jericho.

God's marvelous grace is demonstrated by the change in the life of Rahab. She left the old life behind and embraced the God of Abraham, Isaac, and Jacob. She married Salmon and became the mother of Boaz, who married Ruth. From that union a son, Obed, was born who became the father of Jesse, who would be the father of David, of whose line our Savior was born. God took a woman who was living in a cesspool of sin and placed her in the lineage of the King of kings!

What a glorious picture of redemption we find in the life of Rahab, the former harlot. This is one woman who began in sin and disgrace but finished her race with her light shining brightly.

Bathsheba

We are introduced to Bathsheba in 2 Samuel 11. I have often pondered if she was a willing participant in the sin with King David. Did she deliberately parade herself on the rooftop, bathing in full view of the palace so David would notice? Was she a lonely woman who let her sexual desires sway her judgment? Or did she appeal to the king's sense of right and wrong by explaining she was the wife of one of his faithful soldiers? We will never know whether Bathsheba knowingly seduced David or was the victim of her culture. When she was called to the king's chamber, she had no choice but to go to him. Culturally and politically she was expected to answer affirmatively to the demands of the king.

Despite the beginning circumstances, Bathsheba proved to be a woman of great strength. She endured the lust of a king, the murder of her loyal husband, and the grievous death of her innocent baby. Finding the strength to endure the tremendous emotional pain, she eventually gained the respect of the household of David. She birthed and raised the wisest man who ever lived and the successor to the throne of David.

Proverbs 31, the well-known poem ascribed to the most virtuous of all women, was written by King Lemuel for his mother. Some scholars believe Lemuel is another name used by Solomon. If this is the case, then the woman who experienced the depths of sin, was disgraced as an adulteress woman, and conceived a child outside of her marriage was, at the end of her life, considered the most worthy and valuable of all Old Testament women.

Once again, the grace of God is lavishly applied, making changes in a woman's life. It's not how we start our race that counts, it's how we complete it. Bathsheba, even with a wobbly start, crossed the finish line with her faith intact and her light radiantly shining.

Don't Let Others Define You

I want my daughter to know the second way to keep her light shining at the end of her race is to guard against letting others define who she is and what she is to do with her life.

I was watching one of the late night talk shows that typically interviews celebrities. The famous person being showcased that particular evening was a popular singer and accomplished musician. During the conversation, the star told the host, "Every night, when I walk out on the stage, I wonder, 'Is the audience going to love me tonight?'" No wonder this person was given to bouts of depression and substance abuse. The man lived in constant fear of rejection. He had given over the power to determine his worth to a very fickle group of people.

We cannot depend on others, no matter how well meaning they may be, to make us feel good about ourselves. I want my daughter to find her significance in the joy of serving and pleasing God. What she chooses to do may not fit the description of success this world puts forth; however, if she is accomplishing what God has planned for her life, she will experience true fulfillment.

Since Heidi was a little girl, she has blessed people with her beautiful singing voice. Time and time again I have heard individuals encourage her to pursue a career in vocal performance. From the very beginning I have also instructed her: "You do not have to perform in a public arena to use your gift to its fullest capacity. If God gives you children and you sing lullabies to your babies, that's just as important as singing before thousands at Madison Square Garden in New York City. Ultimately, we sing for an audience of One—the Giver of the gift." Perhaps these lyrics will be an encouragement to those who have chosen to serve God and use their talents in a more quiet, less public way.

Then the Light Turns Green

There's not an empty seat in the place
And she's never sounded so good
She loves this crowd, it's a dream come true
She always believed it would

And the soft red glow of the light
Holds her for a while on the stage
Every heart is held captive, this is her moment
Her song leaves them all amazed

Then the light turns green, there's a tap on her shoulder
It's one of her kids, and the concert is over
And she smiles inside, as her song is reviewed
"Mother thanks for the ride…you sing so pretty
We'll see you after school"

One time a long time ago
She dreamed she was on the charts
She saw her name at the top of the list
She dreamed she would be a star

Then somewhere along the way
Love made a change in her plans
But sometimes she still dreams
Like today in the car
As she sings for her biggest fans[17]

Don't Let the Devil Deceive You

I want my daughter to be alert to the schemes of the devil (see Ephesians 6:11). Contrary to what you might have heard, the main goal of Satan is not to make us drink alcohol or use drugs that are destructive to our bodies. It's not to trick us into smoking cigarettes, leaving our lungs heaps of charred, mangled, cancerous tissue. It's not even to snare us into illicit sexual behaviors and relationships outside of marriage causing all kinds of pain and destruction. As deadly as these things may be, the real devastation comes when we allow ourselves to be deceived into living independently of God. If Satan can accomplish this objective, then we are caught in his snare and it will be only a matter of time before our lights go out.

From the very beginning of time, the devil has been whispering in our ears, "You don't need God's help to live your life." This is the message he gave to Eve in the garden (you won't die; you'll be just like God), and it's the same message he gives us today. Second Corinthians 11:3 NKJV says: "But I am afraid that, as the serpent deceived Eve by his craftiness, your minds will be led astray from the simplicity and purity of devotion to Christ."

I want to say to my daughter, "You will never know true peace and happiness living outside of God's strength and His Word."

Trying to live separately from God's assistance is a subtle deception of the enemy. It occurs when we neglect our prayer time with the Lord. When we fail to daily enlist God's presence in every area of our lives, we are in essence saying, "God, I can do this by myself. I don't need your protection and blessing."

This attitude reminds me of a child I once saw in an airport baggage claim area. She was a little girl who was trying to carry her own suitcase. With the load much bigger than the child herself, she stood tugging and pulling on it. It was obvious to all around that she was incapable of managing such a burden. There was no way she was going to be able to carry it alone. Yet in her childish arrogance and willful way she rebuffed her father's attempt to assist her with the suitcase. As he reached down to help her, she screamed at him, "No, daddy, I can do it all by myself!"

There have been times in my own life when, like a foolish child, I have rejected the very help that I needed the most. Yet God, not unlike the loving father in the airport, reached down to me, picked up the load and, with His hand on mine, carried it.

The longer I live, the more I see my need of God's help. I agree with the words of the old hymn written decades ago:

I Need Thee Every Hour

I need Thee every hour, most gracious Lord
No tender voice like Thine can peace afford
I need Thee every hour, stay Thou nearby;
Temptations lose their power when Thou art nigh

I need Thee every hour, in joy or pain;
Come quickly and abide, or life is in vain
I need Thee every hour; teach me Thy will;
and Thy rich promises in me fulfill.

I need Thee every hour, most Holy One;
O make me Thine indeed, Thou blessed Son.

I need Thee, O I need Thee;
Every hour I need Thee;
O bless me now, my Savior
I come to Thee.[18]

Living our lives as though we do not need God's guidance guarantees we will finish the race in the dark. I want Heidi to always remember the words of David in Psalm 18:28-30:

> For You will light my lamp; the Lord my God will enlighten my darkness. For by You I can run against a troop, by my God I can leap over a wall. As for God, His way is perfect; the word of the Lord is proven; He is a shield to all who trust in Him.

Last-Minute Instructions from Mom

If the natural sequence of life transpires, I will not live to see my daughter finish her race. Hopefully, if the Lord tarries, I will leave this world long before my daughter reaches the end of her life. It is for that reason I want to end with words that will live long after I am gone.

Heidi,
I commit you to our heavenly Father
and pray as you finish your race,
that your light will shine brilliantly
now and forever.

"Now to Him who is able to
keep you from stumbling,
and to present you faultless
before the presence of
His glory with exceeding joy,
to God our Savior,
Who alone is wise,
be glory and majesty,
dominion and power,
both now and forever.
Amen."

Jude 24,25 NKJV

Honest Thoughts from Real Moms

I have asked a few friends to share some thoughts in regard to their relationship with their daughters. I appreciate their honesty, their wisdom, and their hearts. You will too.

Along with knowing Christ and sharing heaven when you die, what do you want most for your daughter?

I want my daughter to know freedom from self-accusations. She seems to take everything so seriously that I fear she is losing the joy of living. If she could realize how much God loves her, then she could be free from the stifling pressure she puts on herself to not fail. I want my daughter to allow God to build into her a sense of self-worth based on the fact that God loves her no matter what she does.

I want my daughter to love Jesus with her whole heart, soul, and mind. She is a woman of destiny, and I pray she will reach that destination as she lives in the center of God's will.

I want my daughter to use her talents and abilities to bless others.

I want my daughter to age gracefully and enjoy a long life with her husband. I want her to know the joy of having her children rise up and call her blessed, even as mine have.

I want my daughter to enjoy the blessing of a healthy body. Since I have struggled with my own health problems, I am concerned she might have inherited that weakness. Through my burden of illness and disease I have learned to relish the peace that comes with enjoying soundness of body.

If you could, what would you change about the way you raised your daughter?

I think I would have done a better job as a mother if I would have taken better care of myself, both physically and spiritually. Often I let my "tank" run dry. If I had kept better communication with God, I believe my responses to my children would have been kinder and wiser. In the same way, when I allowed myself to become extremely tired physically, I was left with a disadvantage in dealing with the emotional aspect of family life.

I put a lot of pressure on my daughter to "be somebody." I kept telling her, "You can be anything you want to be." Looking back, I now realize what I was saying was, "Don't let me down. Make me proud of you." Perhaps this was a reflection on my own life and lack of accomplishments. I never felt like I lived up to my potential, and I didn't want her to make the same mistakes. As a result I pushed her when I should have been encouraging her to seek what God wanted her to do. I should have let go of her and let God be the one to direct her life.

I lost my temper a lot when my kids were growing up. Even though I felt they provoked me, I know now I was just taking my frustrations out on them. I have a lot of regrets.

I wasn't saved when we first had our girls. I regret I wasn't a better example for them to follow. Now all I can do is pray that God will correct some of the damage that was done to them when they were younger.

My biggest regret is that I cleaned house instead of holding my children. At the time I thought all my efforts to keep the house perfect were for their benefit. I wanted them to be proud of where they lived because when I was growing up I was ashamed of my home. I never invited friends over to visit because I knew the house was going to be a filthy mess. So I reacted the opposite way and became obsessed with having a spotless home. Why is it so easy to see the truth looking back? My husband kept telling me to "lighten up" and let them be kids. At the time, I couldn't see it. Now I regret all the time I wasted cleaning a house that was already clean. It's difficult, but I have to admit that the time I spent on the housework was for me. If I could go back in time, I would spend more time being with and loving my children—and husband.

If I had it to do over again, I'd pay more attention to my daughter's education. I regret that I didn't finish school myself, but more than that, I wish I had encouraged my daughter to go on to college. It would have been difficult financially, but we could have done it.

My greatest regret is that I was unable to provide an intact family for my daughter. I've worked really hard to make life as good as possible, but a broken home was the one thing I could never fix. As the sole provider, I had to work outside the home, leaving her in the care of other people. I worked long and hard, which left me little time to spend with her. She has turned out to be a lovely young woman, and I appreciate God's grace and ability to make good come out of my mistakes.

In all the hurry of life, I failed to teach my daughter to memorize the Scriptures. We went to church and God was honored in our home, but I could and should have done more to give her a formal, structured knowledge of the Scriptures. She's doing fine, but I feel if she had a firmer foundation in the Bible, she wouldn't wonder about her decisions so much. She never seems to be quite sure if she's doing the right thing.

My daughter is still very young. I want to make sure I learn from the lessons of others and not be left with regrets.

I have gone through a horrible separation and divorce this year. I have watched my girls go through the valley of death and come out the other side still loving God. My oldest girl said, "You and dad gave me a foundation, and it doesn't change because of the circumstances." With all that has gone wrong in my life, something is very right because I see my beautiful girls with moral beliefs and faith that have not been destroyed by the worst Satan has thrown at them. My heart is broken, my trust shattered, my faith tested, but my joy is full. For the Lord has proven Himself faithful to me, and my children are the delight of my life.

Books I Want My Daughter to Read

Anderson, Neil T. *Victory over the Darkness*. Ventura, CA: Regal Books, 1990.

Brestin, Dee. *My Daughter, My Daughter*. Colorado Springs: Chariot Victor Publishing, 1999.

Carter, Les. *Imperative People*. Nashville: Thomas Nelson Publishers, 1991.

Chapian, Marie. *Mothers and Daughters*. Minneapolis: Bethany House Publishers, 1988.

Chapman, Annie. *Letting Go of Anger*. Eugene, OR: Harvest House Publishers, 2010.

———. *Running on Empty (and looking for the nearest exit)*. Minneapolis: Bethany House Publishers, 1995.

———. *Smart Women Keep It Simple*. Minneapolis: Bethany House Publishers, 1992.

———. *What Do I Want?* Nashville: S&A Family, Inc., 1999.

Chapman, Gary. *The Five Love Languages*. Chicago: Northfield Publishing, 1992.

———. *The Other Side of Love*. Chicago: Moody Press, 1999.

Chapman, Steve, and Annie Chapman. *Gifts Your Kids Can't Break*. Minneapolis: Bethany House Publishers, 1990.

———. *Hot Topics for Couples*. Eugene, OR: Harvest House Publishers, 2010.

———. *Married Lovers, Married Friends*. Minneapolis: Bethany House Publishers, 1989.

Cloud, Henry, and John Townsend. *Boundaries*. Grand Rapids, MI: Zondervan Publishers, 1992.

Cobb, Linda. *Talking Dirty Laundry with the Queen of Clean*. New York: Pocket Books, 2001.

Crittenden, Danielle. *What Our Mothers Didn't Tell Us*. New York: Touchstone, 1999.

Fischer, John. *12 Steps for the Recovering Pharisee*. Minneapolis: Bethany House Publishers, 2000.

Freeman, Becky. *Marriage 911*. Nashville: Broadman & Holman Publishers, 1996.

Fuller, Cheri. *When Mothers Pray*. Sisters, OR: Multnomah, 1997.

Gresh, Dannah. *And the Bride Wore White*. Chicago: Moody Press, 1999.

Harley, Willard. *His Needs, Her Needs.* Grand Rapids, MI: Fleming H. Revell, 1986.

Joy, Donald. *Parents, Kids, and Sexual Integrity.* Waco, TX: Word Books, 1988.

Littauer, Florence. *Hope for Hurting Women.* Waco, TX: Word Books, 1985.

Lockyer, Herbert. *All the Women of the Bible.* Grand Rapids, MI: Lamplighter Books, 1991.

Lotz, Anne Graham. *Just Give Me Jesus.* Nashville: Word Publishers, 2000.

Minear, Ralph, and William Proctor. *Kids Who Have Too Much.* Nashville: Thomas Nelson Publishers, 1989.

Omartian, Stormie. *The Power of a Praying® Wife.* Eugene, OR: Harvest House Publishers, 1997.

Rainey, Dennis, and Barbara Rainey. *Building Your Mate's Self-Esteem.* San Bernadino, CA: Here's Life Publishers, 1986.

Ramsey, Dave. *Financial Peace.* Nashville: Lampo Press, 1992.

Schlessinger, Laura. *Ten Stupid Things Women Do to Mess Up Their Lives.* New York: Villard Books, 1994.

Sciacca, Fran. *Wounded Saints.* Grand Rapids, MI: Baker Book House, 1992.

Seamands, David. *Healing for Damaged Emotions.* Wheaton, IL: Victor Books, 1984.

Sledge, Tim. *Making Peace with Your Past.* Nashville: LifeWay Publishers, 1992.

Smiley, Kendra. *Helping Your Kids Make Good Choices.* Ann Arbor, MI: Servant Publishers, 2000.

Stack, Debi. *Martha to the Max.* Chicago: Moody Press, 2000.

Thurman, Chris. *The Lies We Believe.* Nashville: Thomas Nelson Publishers, 1989.

Vernick, Leslie. *The Truth Principle.* Colorado Springs: WaterBrook Press, 2000.

Wilkinson, Bruce. *The Prayer of Jabez.* Sisters, OR: Multnomah Publishers, 2000.

Yancy, Philip. *The Jesus I Never Knew.* Grand Rapids, MI: Zondervan Publishers, 1995.

———. *What's So Amazing About Grace?* Grand Rapids, MI: Zondervan Publishing House, 1997.

Notes

1. "Hope for the Helpless," in Ray C. Stedman, *From Guilt to Glory*, vol. 1 (Portland, OR: Multnomah Press, 1978), p. 244.
2. Tim Sledge, *Making Peace with Your Past* (Nashville: LifeWay Press), p. 22.
3. "To Come into the Presence," lyrics by Mike Hudson, Straightway Music, ASCAAP.
4. Jill Murray, Ph.D., *But I Love Him* (New York: Regan Books, 2000), adapted from pp. 22-31. Used by permission.
5. "The Treasure," lyrics by Steve and Annie Chapman, ©1975. Used by permission.
6. "Watching You," lyrics by Steve Chapman, Times and Seasons Music, BMI © 1995. Used by permission.
7. Willard Harley, *His Needs, Her Needs* (Grand Rapids, MI: Fleming H. Revell, 1988, 2001), p. 107.
8. In my book *Letting Go of Anger* (Harvest House, 2010), I give more time and space to the subject matter of our words and how we use them.
9. "Wednesday's Prayer," lyrics by Steve Chapman © 1998, Times and Seasons Music, BMI. Used by permission.
10. "Incompatibility," lyrics © Steve and Annie Chapman, Times and Seasons Music, BMI. Used by permission.
11. "Cup Filled Up with Love," lyrics © Steve and Annie Chapman, Dawn Treader Music SESAC 1982. Used by permission.
12. "Labor of My Heart," lyrics © Steve Chapman, Times and Seasons Music, BMI 1991. Used by permission.
13. *USA Today,* August 18, 1997. The study involved 527 adolescents.
14. "The Arrow and the Bow," lyrics © Steve Chapman. Used by permission.
15. "A Mother's Touch," lyrics by Steve Chapman © 1993. Used by permission.
16. "She Still Rules Me from the Grave," lyrics © by Steve Chapman, 1997, Times and Seasons Music. Used by permission.
17. "Then the Light Turns Green," lyrics © by Steve Chapman. Times and Seasons Music. BMI 1997. Used by permission.
18. Lyrics by Annie S. Hawks and Robert Lowry, 1872.